ORIGINAL
TRIUMPH
TR4/4A/5/6

ORIGINAL
TRIUMPH
TR4/4A/5/6

by Bill Piggott

Photography by Simon Clay
Edited by Mark Hughes

Front cover
This beautifully restored Signal Red TR4 owned by
Nigel Wiggins is a very early specimen and as such
illustrates various details not found on later TR4s.

Half-title page
This 1970 model year TR6 in Laurel Green is to North
American carburettor specification, and is seen with
owner David Shapiro and partner enjoying life on a
Californian boulevard.

Title page
The TR250, here seen in the striking colour of Valencia
Blue with authentic silver nose stripe, was the North
American carburettor version of the fuel-injected TR5.
This car is owned by Carroll O'Connor's Classics.

Back cover
Robert 'Bert' Bennett's 1974 model year TR6 displays
the impact-absorbing rubber bumper overriders
introduced for later TR6s sold in North America.

Published 1998 by Bay View Books Ltd
The Red House, 25-26 Bridgeland Street
Bideford, Devon EX39 2PZ, UK

Designed by Chris Fayers

ISBN 1 901432 04 1
Printed in China

Contents

Introduction

Back in 1990, when the first edition of *Original Triumph TR* was being planned, prudence dictated that a single volume would have to suffice for all TRs, from TR2 to TR6. Both I and my publishers considered the possibility of producing two separate volumes, one covering the sidescreen cars and the other the TR4-6 models, but we had doubts about the potential market for a pair of books. However, with nearly 20,000 copies of *Original Triumph TR* (including French and German editions) now having been sold, and with the success of the *Original* series of books generally, we now feel justified in producing the fully revised second edition in two volumes.

The first of these, covering the sidescreen TRs (2/3/3A/3B) was published in the spring of 1998, and this volume covers the later TRs up to and including the North American specification TR6s, produced until mid-1976. I should add that TR7s and TR8s are sufficiently different animals to merit coverage elsewhere.

That there would be sufficient additional material to fill an expanded edition was never in doubt. Many new facts and figures have come to light in the past seven years, TR history proving to be a remarkably dynamic subject. A section on tools has been added, as have details of bodyshell numbering, plus more detailed references throughout to both the TR250 and the carburettor TR6. All the other sections have been rewritten, revised and expanded to incorporate the new material, as well as to expunge the inevitable mistakes that had crept in.

I have tried, of course, to be as accurate as possible, but, should errors be apparent, do please point these out. Every effort will be made to correct them in future printings. The responsibility for any errors rests with myself. In my defence, I would state that totally accurate factory records do not and, I suspect, never did exist, so there is always room for doubt, particularly with regard to the exact introduction points of individual specification changes. Standard-Triumph's own published information is sometimes contradictory, and is also to some extent incomplete. Major specification changes sometimes go entirely unrecorded in factory literature at the time of their introduction, gradually 'seeping' into later manuals and parts catalogues by a process of osmosis. This demonstrates how difficult it can be to be categorical about originality. In any event, there is no such thing as a totally original car – rather that some cars are more original than others. I hope this book will enable readers to ensure that their own cars come into the 'more original' category.

Clearly every aspect of production and originality detail of the TR4-6 series cannot be covered in a book of this size, but reproduction parts catalogues, workshop manuals, handbooks, etc, are freely available to assist, and even original items of factory literature can still be found at reasonable prices if one is patient and persistent. We have endeavoured to include (in both words and pictures) all the major points which will concern owners of these cars when they seek to return them to top condition and original specification, but I should emphasise that there is no substitute for inspecting actual cars and talking to their owners. With the proliferation of TR clubs and events throughout the world, this should not be difficult to do, and a potential TR restorer must always make membership of the appropriate club his or her first priority. Learning from the mistakes of others is both instructive and inexpensive! Another point I must stress is that this book is not a 'how to do it' restoration guide – these are available elsewhere. Its designed purpose is to lead the TR restorer through the maze of detailed changes that surround even such relatively unsophisticated cars as the TR series – quite how restorers of today's complex vehicles will get on in another 20 years' time hardly bears considering!

By way of explanation, I should say that the term 'TR6' is to be read throughout the book as including both the fuel injection cars and the North American carburettor cars, unless the context requires otherwise or the contrary is indicated. The TR250 is referred to separately from the TR5 in many places, but where nothing specific is said about the TR250 the reader may assume that the term 'TR5' includes it – I would hope that all differences between the two cars are dealt with somewhere within this book. For

TRs of exceptional originality, whether restored or unrestored, have been chosen to illustrate this book. This TR4A, bought new by Maury Richmond in Switzerland but now resident in California, has never changed hands and remains largely unaltered.

clarity, 'L', 'O', 'U' and 'P' suffixes have been omitted from commission numbers where they might cause confusion and are otherwise not relevant to the context.

The information contained in the following pages, some of it previously unpublished, is drawn from a wide variety of sources, principal among these being the records of the British Motor Industry Heritage Trust held in its archives at the Heritage Motor Centre, Gaydon, Warwickshire. The TR Register Archives at the club office in Didcot, Oxfordshire, have also proved immensely informative, and a bibliography listing other reference sources can be found at the end of the book. Whenever possible, cars in original condition that have not undergone any major restoration work have been used, even if this dictates that their condition is not quite that of a newly-restored 'concours' car. Inevitably, however, it has not proved possible to illustrate all aspects of TR originality using only unrebuilt cars, so some restored vehicles are also depicted, although these were carefully selected to be as authentic as possible.

As to the cars themselves, thanks are due to the following owners for generously allowing their vehicles to be photographed for this new edition: Nigel Wiggins (Signal Red TR4), David Squance (Powder Blue TR4), Maury Richmond (New White TR4A, owned from new), Carroll O'Connor (Valencia Blue TR250), Steve Mills (Signal Red TR5), David Shapiro (Laurel Green TR6), Dave Lewis (Sapphire Blue TR6), Michael Holden (Pimento Red TR6, owned from nearly new), Robert 'Bert' Bennett (Triumph Racing Green TR6) and Carol Oppenheimer (Pimento Red TR6, owned from new). Thanks are also due

to those several people who responded to my request for original cars but whose vehicles we were unable to use. At this point I must also express my thanks and appreciation to the photographer, Simon Clay, for so ably carrying out his brief on both sides of the Atlantic and for providing wonderfully detailed photographs of all aspects of this range of TRs. A few photographs have been used from other sources, principally the old edition of *Original Triumph TR* (photographed by Paul Debois) and David Hodges' *Essential Triumph TR* (photographed by Graham Lowe). These include cars owned by Derek Pollock (British Racing Green TR4), David Bishop (Signal Red Dove GTR4) and Eric Barrett (Pimento Red TR6, owned from new).

Although I have been the principal Registrar of the TR Register for almost 20 years now, as well as holding the post of Register Archivist for the past five years, I am neither a professional writer nor a professional car restorer. Consequently, I have drawn on the assistance of many other people knowledgeable in TR matters to help me with this book, and credit must be given to them.

First, for all his help generally, and particularly in allowing me and other TR Registrars free access to the TR build records, I thank Anders Ditlev Clausager, Archivist of the British Motor Industry Heritage Trust, and his staff. Next I must thank three of the Registrars of the TR Register, all volunteers who give freely of their valuable time to the club, and also contributed to this book: they are Roger Ferris (TR5/250 Registrar), Derek Graham (TR6 Registrar) and Jon Marshall (TR4/4A Registrar). Their assistance in reporting facts that they have uncovered and in checking my work was invaluable. Thank you, gentlemen!

Others who have assisted include Nigel Wiggins, Mike Hazlewood, Bob Kemp, Dave Lewis, Graham Robson, Patrick van Houtven, Neil Hawtin, Martin Lodawer and, of course, Rosy Good, the tireless General Manager of the TR Register, together with her excellent staff at the club's Didcot headquarters. Finally, I must thank Karen Nadin for her help in typing and arranging the manuscript and captions.

Writing on such a complex subject as car production and specification teaches one not to be categorical. Even though I have done all I can to make this book as accurate and comprehensive as possible within the limitations of the space available, no doubt further details will yet come to light to ensure that even this volume is not definitive. However, if this book's publication leads to more TRs being rescued, restored and above all driven, then it will have been worthwhile.

Bill Piggott
Nottingham

TRs Past & Present

The TR series of sports cars grew from the modest origins of the marriage of an essentially pre-war saloon car chassis with a torquey engine destined to power a tractor. To say that this is an oversimplification is an understatement, yet this is how the first prototype was basically cobbled together early in 1952.

At the head of Standard-Triumph in the post-war period was Sir John Black, an industrialist of the traditional, autocratic type. He knew what he wanted and he wanted it yesterday! Sir John wanted a sports model in his range of cars, and Sir John would not be beaten. William Lyons had produced his Jaguar XK120 and Nuffield was doing well with the MG 'T' types; both these models were fully capable of race and rally success. However, Black's first attempt to enter the lucrative, dollar-earning, sports car market had resulted in the Triumph 1800/2000 Roadster. This car was more in the tradition of the pre-war *boulevardiers*

– lots of show and not much go. It was a worthy and interesting vehicle, but not a sports car. It had virtually no competition success and did not earn many dollars, so Black tried unsuccessfully to purchase the Morgan Car Company.

Morgan, of course, already produced the traditional type of sports car, but eventually, after much negotiation, no deal could be struck, although the company was still permitted to use the Standard Vanguard engine to power its cars. Soon, a second attempt to produce an in-house design was made by Standard-Triumph, this resulting in the 'TRX' Roadster, colloquially known as the 'Bullet'. Regrettably, this over-complex machine was no more of a sports car than the Roadster, and the project was cancelled after a period of vacillation. As 1952 opened, Black was no nearer the creation of his sports model than he had been in 1946.

However, a competition-minded amateur, Ken Rawlings, had shown the way by designing and

This Powder Blue TR4 (CT 6008), owned by David Squance, still carries its original Coventry 'VC' registration number. This same colour was chosen for the 1962 team of four works competition TR4s, which were registered in the sequence 3 VC to 6 VC. Correct 'tripod' headlamps and optional sun visors are seen, but 72-spoke chrome wire wheels were not available in the TR4 period.

This very early TR4 (CT 666L) was originally built as a left-hand drive car, as were virtually all the 1961 TR4s, but has been expertly converted to right-hand drive and fully restored. The owner, Nigel Wiggins, has taken much trouble to ensure that various features unique to the earliest TR4s have been preserved. The absence of a 'TR4' boot badge is quite correct on the earliest cars, while twin period reversing lights and a chromed tail pipe finisher are in evidence.

building a sports car using largely Standard-Triumph components, including the Vanguard engine. Both Sir John Black and his successor Alick Dick contended later that neither they, nor any other Directors, were aware of this car at the time, but recollections of former employees and circumstantial evidence now indicates otherwise. Indeed, Black may have had a direct hand in ensuring that Rawlings received the parts he needed in those days of post-war shortage. Whatever the truth, Rawlings' car, nicknamed 'Buttercup', was most successful, and Standard-Triumph followed the same formula in 1952 – a Vanguard engine in a lightweight chassis clothed with a two-seater body. Costs had to be kept low, for large-scale production was not envisaged. In-house parts were to be used where possible, and body styling had to be simple – compound curves were avoided – to keep down tooling costs. Harry Webster was the firm's chief designer given overall responsibility for creating the new Triumph Sports, and Walter Belgrove was the chief stylist, charged with designing the bodywork. Time was very short, as Black wanted the prototype to be on the stand at the 1952 Earls Court Motor Show, held in October.

A chassis based on a modified Standard 'Flying 9' item was used, with a rear axle and front suspension from the Triumph Mayflower saloon. The Vanguard engine received moderate development, including the fitting of twin SU carburettors. A four-speed version of the Vanguard gearbox was used. A full-width two-seater body with bolt-on external panels was produced, but this had such traditional sports features as cut-away doors and a spare wheel fitted externally on the sloping tail section.

Only the one Triumph Sports '20 TS' prototype existed when the car was revealed to the public at the 1952 Motor Show; it had covered very few miles, and was apparently not even fully completed! Its debut, however, was overshadowed by the sensationally beautiful Healey 100 sports, which had not only clocked-up hundreds of test miles, but had already been enthusiastically road-tested by *Autosport*. The Triumph attracted reasonable interest and quite a few tentative orders, but it was hardly a show-stopper. Following an equally lukewarm reception from the motoring press when they were allowed to try the prototype after the show, Sir John Black asked Ken Richardson, a development engineer and test driver formerly with BRM, to try it.

Richardson knew a bad car when he tried one – and the new Triumph was bad. Somewhat surprisingly, Black accepted Richardson's forthright opinion and asked him to join the company to help develop the car to what it should have been. Thus the historic TR2 was created by Standard-Triumph's dedicated team of designers and engineers during the winter of 1952/3, finally being displayed to the public at the Geneva Motor Show in March 1953 after an intensive four-month development period. The story of how this was achieved has been told many times, and I would refer interested readers to this book's companion volume *Original TR2/3/3A* and to my other TR books to learn more about what have now collectively become known as the 'sidescreen TRs'.

The TR2 soon became a very successful sports car, both in rallies and on the race track, as well as being eminently practical for everyday use. It was developed into the TR3 towards the end of 1955, and in October 1956 the TR3 became the world's first series production car to be fitted with disc brakes. By late 1957 the TR3A version arrived and the car became a major hit in export markets, with around 90% of production being exported, largely to the USA. The sidescreen TR also became arguably the most successful rally car of the late '50s, both at international and club levels, and modified racing versions with twin-cam engines showed well at Le Mans in 1959, '60 and '61. The factory's competition department, instituted in 1954 under Ken Richardson's guidance, was a force to be reckoned with until summarily shut down as a result of the Leyland take-over of Standard-Triumph in 1961. The other significant event in the TR story in 1961 was the launch of the first of the cars dealt with in the present volume – the TR4.

Although more than 80,000 sidescreen TRs had been produced by 1961, the sports car market was perceived to be moving away from the traditional open two-seater with cut-away doors and vestigial weather protection, however successful it had been. The '60s buyer required more sophisticated transport, a car still encompassing most of the traditional sports car virtues such as speed and ruggedness, yet with modern comforts such as winding glass windows, a heater that worked, and so on. Fortunately, Standard-Triumph had foreseen this trend and design work on the TR3A's successor had begun in 1958, thus allowing the launch of the TR4 in the autumn of 1961, at a time when sales of the TR3A were finally beginning to run out of steam.

Through this period the company was in serious financial difficulty. The development costs of the Triumph Herald and the TR4 together, coupled with a national recession and industrial unrest, meant that Standard-Triumph was barely surviving. Indeed had it not been for the Leyland Group take-over during 1961, there may well have been no subsequent TRs, an illustrious line of British sports cars ending in the still-birth of the TR4. Luckily, financial rescue came just in time, and the TR4 was launched to public acclaim, with

This TR4A (CTC 52847L) correctly displays painted 60-spoke wire wheels, as well as the new sidelight/ indicator style, chromed side strip and grille introduced for this model. Owned from new by Maury Richmond, it has an international history appropriate to its mixed registrations. At the front it sports a UK plate, but at the rear, as can be seen elsewhere, is a Californian one...

waiting lists soon arising at home, particularly as production for the first six months was mainly directed to the USA to earn much-needed cash as quickly as possible.

The brief for the body design of the TR4 had gone to Michelotti in Italy, a designer who had a profound influence on the company's products during the '60s, and indirectly on styling trends throughout the British motor industry. Michelotti created a classic and timeless shape which remains both smart and modern-looking today, and which continued in production with only detailed changes until almost the end of the '60s. It was both stylish and practical, two factors not always easy to combine, and the addition of the innovative 'Surrey' hard-top only served to enhance both

attributes. The new shape, of course, was seen as the TR3A successor's major selling point, for Triumph's engineers and salesmen considered that there was still sufficient life left in the previous TR's chassis design and mechanical components. In any event, the money to have allowed these areas to be completely revised at the same time as the body simply was not available.

The new body was mounted on a chassis that was in effect a TR3A chassis modified only so far as was necessary to mount the heavier, wider body, together with the long overdue rack and pinion steering system. Other mechanical improvements included the standardisation of the formerly optional 2138cc engine, plus the incorporation of synchromesh on first gear. These two changes also appeared in the short-lived TR3B, a revival of the TR3A produced exclusively for the North American market at the behest of Triumph's US distributors during 1962 – a surprising 'last gasp' for the rugged brigade. TR3A brakes and suspension were carried over almost unaltered to the TR4, as were many other minor items – even the seats of the earlier TR4s came from the sidescreen car.

Press reaction to the new Triumph was largely favourable. The introductory UK price of £1032 (including tax) for the basic car was considered good value, but there were some moans about the 'antiquated' rear suspension, which perpetuated the earlier TR's problems with limited axle movement. Triumph's engineers had been working on various designs of independent rear suspension (IRS) systems since about 1957, but cost to the customer and complexity, plus the company's own financial position and the need to have the TR4 on sale as soon as possible, led to it being postponed for a further 3½ years. The rack and pinion steering came in for high praise – anyone used to the sidescreen car's heavy and vague system would have found it delightful. The new body and clever hard-top received much commendation.

Looking back 35 years, the TR4 can be considered a success both as a car and as a commercial venture in all important respects bar one. The one aspect which showed no improvement over the earlier cars was the performance. Although engine power was slightly increased, weight was also up and the frontal area was bigger. However, this comparative lack of urge did not appear to affect sales figures, and the revived competition department showed in 1962 that the TR4 could be modified to 'go a bit' should owners so desire.

A team of works TR4s was campaigned in many international events during the 1962 and '63 seasons, extending to '64 when three of the cars were sent to a major rally in North America, following which they were sold off there, the works competition department never again using TRs in motor sport. Indeed, it seemed by the mid-'60s that the four-cylinder engine was reaching the end of its development, which was leading to the TR4s becoming uncompetitive in European events, although development work still continued on racing TRs in the USA. Indeed, wonders have subsequently been worked with this engine, outputs of up to 200bhp having been achieved in the '90s. The rise of the modified saloon, particularly the Mini Cooper, brought about the demise of the traditional sporting two-seater rally car, which was always at a disadvantage as regards ground clearance once the major rallies took to the forests in the early '60s, and by 1964 the TR had really ceased to be a force in European competition. Some private owners campaigned substantially modified TR4s in amateur events in

Britain, but very few of the later independent rear suspension TRs were used competitively in their day other than in the USA.

By the middle of the decade, comfort and technological advance were becoming very marketable qualities even in traditional sports cars, so the time had come for an independent rear suspension system to be added to the TR. Triumph had a reputation for technical innovation – the Herald was the first British popular car with all-round independent springing – but the engineers felt that something more sophisticated than the Herald's swing-axle system was required for the much more powerful TR, so a coil spring arrangement with trailing arm type wishbones was adopted. This gave considerably increased grip at the rear, together with a softer ride and greater comfort. A new chassis design was required, but most mechanical parts for the new IRS car, called the TR4A, were carried over from the TR4. Only detail changes were made to the bodywork, while engine output was slightly uprated.

Launched early in 1965, the revised TR impressed contemporary road testers with its new suspension, which contributed to improved handling and roadholding, although a certain amount of the predicable 'chuckability' of the old solid-axle TRs had gone. Despite the TR4A's generally favourable reception, penalties of cost and complexity associated with the IRS system led to the company's North American distributors once again demanding (and getting) a model specific to their market – the live-axle TR4A. They felt that many US buyers would prefer the cheaper, rigid-axle rear end, so the new IRS chassis was adapted to carry cart springs and a conventional rear axle. This version of the TR4A was sold in North America alongside the IRS car, IRS being in effect an 'optional extra'. US brochures helpfully pointed out that this 'extra' could not be added following delivery of the car!

One minor feature of the TR4/4A story not so far mentioned concerns the 'GTR4 Dove', to give it its proper nomenclature. This attempt at providing TR buyers with genuine 2+2 accommodation pre-dated the MGB GT by two years, although, unfortunately, it was nothing like as successful commercially. L. F. Dove and Co of Wimbledon, South London, had been Triumph agents for many years, specialising in TRs throughout the '50s. Once the TR4 was on sale, they had coachbuilders Harringtons set to work on one, converting it into a sort of fastback saloon with tail hatch, with two reasonably sized rear seats for the 'family man' and his entourage. In practical terms, the car was effective, despite somewhat ungainly looks, but there was a large price premium over the standard car and fewer than 100 were sold. A section on the Dove, which

This rare GTR4 Dove coupé belonging to David Bishop is one of only a few such cars currently in running order. The low angle emphasises the massive look of the cabin area, which contains an opening tailgate.

was available on both the TR4 and TR4A chassis, will be found on pages 105-108.

Once the TR's handling had been modernised with the TR4A's IRS system, Triumph's engineers were left with the car's relative lack of urge. The 1965 TR4A produced performance figures that were really no better than those of the 1953 TR2, and what had once been a sports car in the very front rank for speed and acceleration had become only average, many contemporary saloons being capable of outrunning a TR4A. Indeed, Triumph's own 2-litre Vitesse saloon of 1966 turned in very similar figures! In retrospect, the TR4A can be seen as something of a 'stop-gap' model, and it was not quite the sales success that the earlier cars had been. Clearly, some urgent action was again needed to revive sales, and this was taken in the form of further 'stop-gap' models, the TR5 and TR250, which arrived in the autumn of 1967.

A 2.5-litre six-cylinder engine was developed for these cars, and when fitted with Lucas fuel injection, as it was in TR5 form, it promptly produced 150bhp. Emissions legislation in the USA meant that the TR250 had twin carburettors rather than fuel injection, and was consequently considerably slower. The TR5's use of fuel injection, a first in a British production car, further enhanced Triumph's reputation for innovation. This engine more than answered the previous criticisms, the TR5 becoming the fastest TR so far, and a match for much more expensive and exotic cars. The price (including tax) of the basic TR5 was £1212 – exceptional value for such a fast car. The old TR4/4A body had to suffice, however, with the usual minor 'facelift' adjustments, for nothing new was ready, and Triumph's Leyland masters were not themselves in a position to expend cash on a totally retooled body for a relatively low production car. This problem did not evaporate, despite the huge performance uplift that the non-US TR had received. From a sales and marketing point of view, new bodywork was still an urgent necessity, and this difficulty was fortunately solved during 1968, ingeniously, rapidly and at minimum cost.

Although modified saloons had continued to chip away at the traditional sports car market in Europe, open two-seater sales were still strong in the USA, Canada and Australasia. The company therefore considered that sufficient potential was left in the TR concept to justify further expenditure on updated bodywork. As is well-known, the German coachbuilding firm of Karmann was instructed to update the existing body as quickly as possible, and with minimal disturbance to the basic structure. Karmann met the near impossible time scale imposed upon them and produced the TR6. The new style cleverly retained the existing central section (including windscreen and doors) and inner structures, but with new wings, bonnet, boot, front and rear panels and external trim. A smart and weatherproof steel hard-top was also designed, although this was now a one-piece item, the previous lift-off central panel having been abandoned. The resulting car looked handsome and modern, and, more importantly, was ready for production in late 1968, after a gestation period of barely a year, allowing the TR5/250 series to be superseded after it had been in production for only 15 months.

Seen to good effect in this high view of Carroll O'Connor's superb TR250 (CD 6037L) is the reflective bonnet stripe that was unique to this North American model with the new six-cylinder engine in carburettor form. As with the parallel TR5, the offset position of the front badge was supposed to create an illusion of greater width. A 'Surrey' top and period luggage rack are fitted.

This superb example of the rare fuel injection TR5 is CP 2780, owned by Steve Mills. Compared with the TR4A, revised exterior details for the six-cylinder version include a modernised grille, matt black sills, a bright sill trim strip and prominent tail badging. The stylish and practical 'Surrey' top, which was such an innovative feature, is seen with the steel roof panel both fitted and removed.

With its excellent performance and updated looks, the fuel injected TR6 sold strongly everywhere except in North America, where the injected engine still could not be made to meet environmental legislation economically. The North American market again received a much slower version with twin carburettors, although, unlike the TR250, no different name was adopted. Despite this, the 'Federal' TR6 sold surprisingly well, and continued to be produced and sold for

David Shapiro's 1970 TR6 (CC 53568L) looks superb in the uncommon colour of Laurel Green. The standard US fitting of 185-section tyres, here with period red bands on the sidewalls, give the whole vehicle a larger look, as well as raising the

ride height. As with so many cars, the octagonal wheel nuts for the 72-spoke wire wheels have been replaced by the racier 'knock-off' variety. The Light Tan seats have head restraints, which were fitted to all US-market carburettor TR6s.

some time after its injected sister car had been deleted, notwithstanding the fact that in its final form the acceleration could not, in most respects, even match that of the TR2 of more than 20 years earlier!

The TR6 remained in production longer than any previous TR model, but by the latter stages it was inevitably becoming an anachronism and sales eventually slowed. The company saw no reason to commit further funds in a vain attempt to keep alive a concept whose time had apparently passed, and hence the TR family rather faded away. The last fuel injected TR6 was made in February 1975, while production of the 'Federal' car staggered on in strangulated form until July 1976. Evidently these last cars were available well into 1977, gracing US showrooms with large discount stickers in their windscreens!

Looking back from the '90s, maybe the subsequent reputation of the TR series would have been better served had production ceased in the early

Eric Barrett still owns this exceptional TR6 (right), which he bought new with the optional hard-top. The low camera angle emphasises the purposeful look of the car. Detail changes for the 1973 model year included silver wheel centres and bright trim at the top and bottom of the grille. As a UK-specification car, the sidelight sections of its light units are uncoloured, and the black windscreen frame – found on all TR6s except those of the 1969 model year – shows up well against Pimento Red paint.

Dave Lewis's concours-winning TR6 (CP 75552) looks superb, particularly with the soft-top folded and the neat cover in place. Apparent from this angle is the normal negative camber on the rear wheels, which are the standard disc version with centres in the earlier black finish. This 1972 model year car, still with the fuel injection engine in 150bhp form, arguably represents the pinnacle of TR design.

'70s, before emasculation took place, for even the injected cars were detuned from 150bhp to 125bhp for the 1973 model year. Can one blame the company, however, for trying to extract the final financial knockings from what had been for more than 20 years one of the world's most successful series of sports cars?

Turning to view the TR scene nowadays, one cannot say that it looks other than healthy. Values rose steadily throughout the '80s and held up well during the recession of the early '90s. In fact, possibly because they were not as highly priced as many other classic two-seaters, TRs remained the choice of the enthusiast rather than the speculator during the boom years, which has very much benefited both the cars and the stability of their values. The TR in all its forms remains excellent value for money, and is mercifully free from the 'hype' that surrounds some classic roadsters.

This stability of value has had the beneficial effect of making restoration more cost-effective, which in turn has led to a proliferation of specialist firms dealing with TR parts and restoration. The parts supply situation for all models is extremely good, parts unique to the Dove conversions being the only exception. Almost all body panels, mechanical and chassis parts are generally available, even complete new chassis, and, from the Heritage organisation, complete panelled TR6 bodyshells! Inevitably there can be brief periods when there are temporary stock shortages, but overall it is little exaggeration to say that it would now be possible to create in all substantial respects a brand new TR6 (for instance) from scratch!

This is all very different from the situation 15 to 20 years ago, when the TR4-6 cars were often just scruffy old sports cars being run into the

Robert 'Bert' Bennett's TR6 (CF 16305U) dates from the 1974 model year, the first for the '5mph impact safety bumpers' that did little for the looks of US models. The colour, Triumph Racing Green, is very similar to the earlier Laurel Green. The Chestnut trim is rare but correct. Knock-off wheel nuts, again, have replaced the octagonal ones.

Carol Oppenheimer's beautifully preserved 1976 model year Pimento Red TR6 (CF 50871U), owned by her from new, shows its 'high-line' US bumpers, which required the sidelight/indicator units to be hung below. The wheels wear period options of polished alloy rim embellishers and red-band tyres that were fitted to so many US cars. Other US-only features are reflective edging for the soft-top and the 'Union Flag' rear wing decals of later models.

ground by the impecunious, parts being provided in many cases by cannibalising similar cars because factory spares support had ceased, and many of today's specialists had yet to arrive. The TR renaissance has been greatly assisted by the principal club for these cars, the TR Register, founded in 1970 initially to cater for the sidescreen TRs, but covering for more than 20 years now the cars dealt with in this book. The TR Register is now one of the world's largest one-make car clubs, and acts as a support group for TR enthusiasts world-wide, being run from permanent headquarters by a combination of professional staff and volunteers in Didcot, Oxfordshire.

The TR competition motoring scene is also extremely healthy, the six-cylinder cars being raced today in the UK in a way in which they rarely were in their youth. The TR Register's season of 'TR only' races attracts full grids year

after year, and ensures that one of the purposes behind the whole TR series is still fulfilled, that of providing sporting and competitive motoring at moderate cost. In addition, during the '90s, the strong growth of the historic rallying movement has not surprisingly encompassed TRs. Several of the top historic rally cars, even at international level, are TR4s, and additionally three out of the four ex-works competition TR4s have been fully restored, not just as museum pieces, but as competitive rally cars.

It is today possible to restore any TR to a very high standard of both originality and condition. However, be warned that this can never be an inexpensive exercise. At today's values, the cost of such restoration will normally exceed the value of the completed car. However, the fun to be had from the finished product makes it all worthwhile, even if the exercise is not a route to a quick profit.

Body & Exterior Trim

As had been the case with the bodywork construction of earlier TRs, much use was made of bolt-on outer panels – a considerable advantage to the home restorer today. The inner structure was built up from a multiplicity of separate pressed panels, all welded into a cohesive unit and mounted onto the strong separate chassis frame. When rebuilding a TR body, especially one weakened by rust, note that it can collapse about the centre section when removed from the chassis, so suitable precautions should be taken. Fitting temporary supports across the top of the door openings is a good idea.

The body was constructed mainly from pressed 19 or 20 swg (0.043 in or 0.035 in) steel, aluminium being employed only for the Surrey top's cast rear window surround and early pattern of hard-top centre section. The central core of the body was formed by the front bulkhead/scuttle assembly, front inner wings and wheel arches, floors either side, inner and outer sill sections, quarter panels, A and B posts, rear floor and prop shaft tunnel sections, rear inner wings and wheel arch sections, rear deck assembly, boot floor pan, boot side panels and rear valance panel, together with a number of smaller closing panels and brackets.

This whole assembly was built up at Triumph's then new production facility at Speke near Liverpool, where outer panels were also added and the assembled structure was fully painted in body colour. Most of the interior trim also went in at this stage, only seats and carpets remaining to be fitted after the bodies had been transported by road to the Coventry plant. There the bodies were united with their chassis, mechanical and electrical components were installed, and final fitting out, inspection and rectification took place. TR250 and TR5 bodies were manufactured with lifting eyes fitted to the front inner wings, to facilitate transport within the factory. These were absent from TR4/4A bodies, and also not fitted to 'Stanpart' replacement inner wings for any of these cars, so their presence is a good indicator of a car's originality.

Bodies of TR4/4A/5/250 models were very similar to each other. Although at first glance the TR6 body appears quite different, in reality it was a clever facelift performed in double-quick time by the German firm of Karmann. The central and inner sections remained almost the same, the

One of the great families of British sports cars had continental styling roots. Broadside views show how the timeless lines created by Michelotti of Italy for the TR4 (below) were cleverly updated by Karmann of Germany for the TR6 (facing page). The later car's nose and tail revisions brought a very different look, even though the central section was basically unchanged.

The life-span of the Michelotti-bodied cars saw five bonnet specifications with differing details, but the most visible change was in the profile of the bulge required to clear the carburettors. A 'short' bulge (right), stopping several inches before the bonnet's trailing edge, was found on early TR4s. The more familiar 'long' bulge (far right) arrived at CT 6429 and continued through to the end of TR5/250 production, even though it was redundant on the injected TR5.

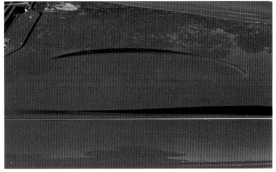
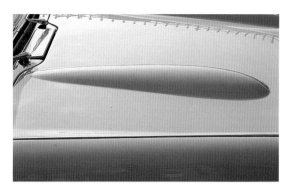

facelift being effected by new wings, bonnet, boot, front/rear panels and valances. For this reason it is convenient to regard all the TR models in this book as the same from the body point of view.

A front-hinged bonnet with internal hinges was used for the first time on the TR4, immeasurably improving access to the radiator area and making engine removal much easier. An internal release mechanism was used for the bonnet, with the catch assembly mounted on the bulkhead on the carburettor side of the engine. The bonnet of the TR4/4A needed a 'power bulge' to clear the carburettor tops and allow for engine movement, and this feature remained as a nice irrelevance for the TR5 although its necessity disappeared with the adoption of fuel injection. In fact, there were five different TR4/4A/5/250 bonnets. The first type (part number 950121), fitted up to CT 6429, had a short power bulge which stopped about 4in from the back edge of the bonnet. The second type (part number 903178), fitted from CT 6430 to body number 37689 CT, had the more familiar long power bulge, extending right to the rear of the bonnet; this bonnet was otherwise very similar to the earlier one apart from slight differences in

some stiffening members. The rear corners of both of these bonnets lacked the sockets fitted to later cars to engage with the conical rubber adjustable locating pins, the underside of the bonnet merely being held against buffer pads by the action of the spring bonnet catch. The third type of bonnet (part number 904130), fitted to late TR4s from body number 37690 CT and to all TR4As, differed from the second type in two respects: not only did this bonnet incorporate sockets to mate with the locating pins, but the stiffening members on the underside differed, evidently to allow the bonnet to clear the TR4A's redesigned radiator. The fourth type of bonnet (part number 908031), that of the TR5/250, differed from the third type only in that it was pierced in a different place for the front badge and had no holes for the now-deleted 'Triumph' lettering. Finally, Triumph rationalised the spares supply position by producing a fifth type of 'universal' bonnet which covered all models – this had sockets, the long power bulge and no drillings for badges. The TR6 bonnet was unique to the model and there was only one type. All bonnets were manually propped by a black-painted 'bent-wire' prop

To subdue scuttle shake, this console bracket, seen on an early TR4, connected the dashboard to the floors. When no radio was fitted, the upper section was trimmed in vinyl, as here.

mounted on the bonnet and engaging in a holder on top of the offside front wheel arch.

Wings on the TR4/4A/5 models did not vary, with the exception of drillings for differing external trim and lighting arrangements; TR6 wings were again unique to the model. Doors were also broadly similar, this time throughout the range, but they differed in detail regarding locks, handles and internal and external trim. A little-known fact is that there were two types of TR4 door, changing at body number 22343 CT. The difference is in the check straps, the earlier type being vertically installed, the later type horizontal; an associated small change in the A post was also necessary. Late TR6 doors were fitted with side impact bars, but the complete door remained interchangeable with the earlier TR6 version. The winding windows fitted to all these cars were of a frameless design that can cause sealing and alignment problems. Door glasses remained the same throughout, but the raising and lowering mechanism was changed. The earlier 'scissors' type found on the TR4 and TR4A was not entirely satisfactory in use, so there was a different design for the later cars. The two-piece A post and B post were also broadly similar, altering throughout the range only in detail. The latch plate on each B post was always of anti-burst design, but the TR4/4A type used a separate tongue and latch

whereas the TR5/250/6 type was an integrated unit.

An inner and outer sill assembly, with a filler piece at each end, was fitted to these cars, the sill being welded to brackets which bolted to the floor and chassis. Floors were ribbed pressings, and minor changes were made to these and to the transmission tunnel and propeller shaft cover from the TR4A onwards because of a revised handbrake position. Surprisingly, the holes in the floors used for the TR4-type jack remained to puzzle owners of later TRs!

The rear bulkhead was built up from a deck assembly spanning the area behind the cockpit, a tonneau panel on each side, and the rear inner wings (to which separate wheel arch panels were welded). From TR4 number CT 5643, the rear deck assembly was made in three pieces instead of one. Between the wheel arches was a pressed occasional rear seat pan and a vertical heel board connecting to the rear of the transmission tunnel. The forward end of the transmission was covered by a bolted-in gearbox cover, similar to that of the TR3A but now made in pressure-moulded fibreboard to improve sound-deadening. Since some rigidity was lost by this piece no longer being in steel, an H-shaped console bracket connected the dashboard to the floors and chassis, straddling the gearbox cover. Prototypes had no such bracket, but scuttle shake and the need for radio fitment led to it quickly being introduced. The early bracket, which was only fitted up to CT 1527, was slightly differently shaped, having a cut-out at the top, and was also covered in black vinyl, whereas the later bracket was painted in a black 'crackle' finish. Cars for the USA had this bracket further modified in both January and March 1962, vinyl covering being introduced for a brief period.

At the rear, the spare wheel sat in a sheet steel pan to which were welded stepped side floors with welded brackets to bolt to the chassis. The rear of the car was completed by a valance, which was welded at the top on both sides to the side tonneau panels, the boot aperture thus being formed. Steel housings for the rear light units were welded to the inner wings and the bolted-on outer rear wings closed over them. The boot lid had chromed external hinges and a bolted-on internal framework for strength. This framework was reinforced at the same time as the rear deck became a three-piece assembly, from car number CT 5643. The boot lid on early TR4s was supported by a manual prop, rather like the one used for the bonnet, but this was soon replaced – again at car number CT 5643 – by a self-propping stay, which was fitted on the left-hand side looking from the rear and usually left unpainted. The 'catch bracket' required to engage the manual prop was a further difference in the early one-piece deck assembly.

At the front of the body was a two-piece

Continuous styling evolution shown in front views, from top left. 1) TR4 grille was pressed from polished aluminium, and contained both indicators and sidelights. This early TR4 has the very rare starting handle option: the chromed bracket for the handle can be seen bolted to the top of the bumper, with blanking plug installed. 2) TR4A grille changed to bold horizontal bars with a central upright, and sidelights moved to the front wings. Clearly visible is the hole in grille and valance for the starting handle, even though this was by now redundant, there being no hole in the radiator. 3) The TR5 grille, like TR250's, evolved a little further, with matt black paint on the upward-facing surfaces of the horizontal bars. The starting handle aperture had finally disappeared, although the corresponding front valance cut-out still remained! 4) TR6 grille, seen on a US car (note all-amber sidelight/indicator units) from the 1970 model year, had black plastic 'chip-cutter' style with a bright central bar. 5) Introduction of CR/CF series TR6s for the 1973 model year brought stainless steel beading for the top and bottom of the grille, and rubber overriders came a year later for US models. 6) Grille was unchanged for 1975 and 1976 model years, but US regulations required higher bumpers, which in turn necessitated repositioned side and indicator light units.

valance. The upper part on the TR4 body had holes for the headlights and starting handle, the lower part a starting handle cut-out. The TR4A's upper valance differed in detail, but the lower valance was unchanged, the starting handle aperture remaining although the handle itself was no longer available. The TR5/250 lower valance gained a central cut-out, presumably for cooling, while the starting handle cut-out continued even though the new grille no longer catered for this. As at the back, inner wings were welded to the wheel arch sections and at their rear ends to a large central bulkhead pressing, which had end panel assemblies closing each side. A separate scuttle assembly in two pieces was welded across the top of the back of the bulkhead to complete the front end of the body. Although the TR5/250 body appears virtually identical to the TR4/4A, there were some detailed structural differences, as well as the obvious trim and decorative ones. For instance, the reinforced ribbed pressings on the horizontal surface of the front bulkhead of the TR4/4A (near the pedal box assembly and wiper motor) were absent on the TR5/250.

Despite its different appearance, the TR6 body was built up in much the same way as that of the Michelotti cars. The near-flat boot lid now had internal hinges and an integral stiffening framework; a fixed rear panel was also incorporated. The front valance was now a one-piece unit with two cooling slots, and the CR/CF series TR6s had a separate black moulded spoiler in addition. This was screwed into place somewhat flimsily, the bumper having to be moved forward slightly to make room for the spoiler and its attachments.

The inner body panel work, floors and areas under the bonnet and the wheel arches should be painted in external body colour on all of these cars.

Door sealing was achieved by a rubber outer seal and an inner draught excluder described in the parts list as 'Snappon' – this appears to have been a development of the old 'Furflex' type of seal. On cars built with 'Surrey' hard-tops, the sealing continued unbroken from the rear of the door aperture up the hard-top frame itself to the top of the door window glass, and also over the top of the leading edge of the hard-top rear window. The trailing edge of the bonnet mated with a rubber seal inserted along the scuttle top, while the boot had a rubber seal all round the aperture. A rubber seal and a separate weather strip were fitted in the tops of the doors.

These cars were manufactured in what was still the 'chrome' period for external body fittings, but the beginnings of the 'matt black' vogue caught up with later TR6s. All models had chromed exterior door handles, those of the TR5/250/6 being slimmer than the TR4/4A ones. Both TR4/4A handles incorporated key locking, whereas the

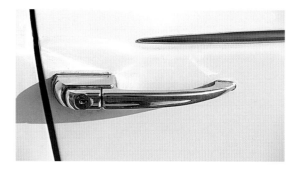

later cars featured a separate lock on each side a couple of inches below the handle. A chromed 'T' boot handle with a lock incorporated was mounted below the number plate on TR4/4A/5/250 models, while the fixed rear panel of the TR6 carried a chromed twist-type lock which caused the lid to spring up from the catch sufficiently to raise it.

The chromed fuel filler cap on the TR4/4A/5 was of the traditional TR quick-release snap-action type, fitted in the centre of the rear deck panel. The hinged cap was released by pressing a chromed tongue, which was meant to point to the driver's side of the car. The TR250 had a 'Monza' style filler cap, larger in diameter than the TR4/4A/5 type and kept closed by magnetic action. It seems from the sales brochures that this 'racing' type of cap was fitted to all TR250s as a selling point, although its heritage was not remotely connected with motor racing – it was actually borrowed from a large Leyland truck! Early injection TR6s still sported the TR4/4A/5 style of cap, but cars from 1970 onwards had a safety cap with the

All of these TRs could be locked externally from both sides of the car, but two patterns of handle and lock were used. The TR4/4A handle had an integral lock in the push button (above left), whereas TR5/250/6 models had the lock separate from a slightly slimmer handle (below left). The chromed side trim, found only on the TR4A/5/250 models, also became thicker with the change from four to six cylinders.

The conventional boot handle used for the TR4/4A/5/ 250 (above left) was replaced for the TR6 by a push-button boot lock (above) mounted on the rear panel rather than the boot lid.

The fuel filler, its central mounting on the rear deck allowing access from either side of the car, came with three styles of cap. The TR4/4A/5 and early injection TR6 filler cap (left) had an exposed release tongue, which should face towards the driver's side of the car. Later injection TR6s had a 'safety' filler cap (middle) with a shielded release lever, to prevent the cap springing open in the event of the car overturning. For the US, TR250s and carburettor TR6s normally had a racing style 'Monza' filler cap (right), reportedly sourced from a Leyland truck!

release button shielded below the cap, so that, should the car overturn, the tongue could not be released by contact with the ground. It is believed that all US specification TR6s had the larger 'Monza' cap as fitted to the TR250.

Chromed bumpers (with black brackets) were fitted to all of these cars. The TR4 had a heavy-duty front bumper, with twin overriders, mounted on substantial brackets bolted to the forward end of the chassis, with extra bracing pieces connecting the overriders to the front wheel arches, and brackets stiffening the bumper internally. If the optional starting handle was specified, a special support bracket for this was bolted to the top of the bumper. The TR4A front bumper's overriders were moved much nearer to the outer ends of the bumper blade, outboard of the headlamps; this necessitated redrilling the original blade. The overriders themselves were shorter, although said to be 'heavier duty', and the stays to the wheel arches were deleted. The bumper itself was raised slightly in relation to that of the TR4. The TR4A front bumper continued for the TR5/250, but the TR6 was given new 'slim-line' bumpers.

There were four versions of TR6 front bumper: the CP/CC 'no spoiler' type, the CR/CF type with a spoiler, the 1974 US type with rubber overriders, and the 1975/76 US type with rubber overriders. Cars from CR1 and CF1 were given extra, more substantial, fixings for their front bumpers, presumably inspired by North American parking habits! The 1975 and '76 model year US TR6s had their front bumpers raised, which required repositioning of the sidelights and indicators. The rubber overriders, although ugly and looking very much an afterthought, at least enabled the later North American TR6s to meet the '5mph' impact tests, and thus allowed the car to be sold for nearly two years longer than would otherwise have been

Unlike the TR6, the Michelotti-bodied cars always had bumper overriders. Those at the front were mounted in a relatively inboard position on the TR4 (right), but moved outwards for the TR4A/5/250 (far right) and became more compact in appearance.

Side-on TR6 views show how dramatically the massive '5mph impact' overriders, added to North American TR6s for the 1974 model year, changed the frontal appearance. The later car should be fitted with a spoiler.

US-specification front overriders, when introduced for 1974, slightly obscured the all-amber sidelight/indicator units (right). When legislation a year later required bumper height to be raised, Triumph was forced to fit different sidelight/indicator units below the bumper (far right).

Three TR6 rear views, showing differing rear bumper styles. The first type (left), used until the end of the 1972 model year, had the number plate light mounted in a raised housing in the centre of the bumper. The second type (centre left) was plain in the centre, with number plate lighting now directed downwards from the top of the panel recess, and US cars for the 1974 model year also received rubber overriders, which concealed the joins in the bumper. The third type of bumper (bottom left), for the US only, was mounted higher and incorporated a 'Triumph' badge on a plinth in the centre.

the case. With the TR7 already nearly available for release, Triumph was not in a position to spend money on a complete redesign of the TR6 front – and in view of what happened to the MGB this was probably just as well! Licence plate plinths were also incorporated into the front bumpers of the later North American TR6s.

The rear bumper was the same on TR4/4A/5/ 250 models. Again, this was a substantial chromed blade with twin overriders, these incorporating the number plate illumination (see 'Electrics & Lamps', page 65). The rear bumper wrapped around the bodywork corners, and consequently was bracketed not only to the chassis at the over-rider mounting area, but also to the ends of the rear chassis cross tube by outriggers attaching to the bumper sides. In addition, further small brackets tied the base of the rear overriders directly to the chassis. Again, the TR6 had a unique rear bumper, a three-piece item formed of a central blade with two corner sections to give side protection. A black joint washer and joint plate was used on each side to connect the three pieces. The central blade attached to the chassis by the usual two substantial brackets, and outriggers to the rear chassis cross tube supported the forward ends of the outer sections. There were four types of TR6 rear bumper central section: one accommodated the earlier number plate light on top of the bumper; a second plain type was used on CR/CF series cars; a third US type appeared to take account of the large rubber overriders first fitted on 1974 model year cars; the fourth type, again with large overriders, was fitted to 1975/76 US cars and had a new 'Triumph' name badge incorporated on a plinth, and also necessitated modified side sections as these were now fixed higher on the body.

All four models used different radiator grilles. The TR4 grille, bearing a family resemblance to the cellular TR3A type, was manufactured from similar pressed, polished aluminium sheet. Secured by stays to the front valance, it incorporated cut-outs for the headlamps, starting handle, sidelamps, flasher units and overrider supports. The TR4A grille was composed of horizontal bars and a single upright inset in the centre. There were two types of TR4A grille: the cross-section of the horizontal bars changed from rounded to a more angular, squared-off shape at an unknown point in production, probably in late 1966 or early 1967. Like the TR4 grille, the TR4A item was a one-piece pressing and the leading edges of the horizontal bars were polished. The TR5 grille was very similar but had matt black paint on the upward-facing surfaces of the horizontal bars, the sharper leading edges of the bars still having the polished aluminium finish, as with the TR4A.

Unlike the TR4A, the bottom horizontal bar was no longer scalloped to clear a starting handle, which had been dispensed with.

The TR6 had a matt black 'chip-cutter' grille made from anodised aluminium. It was inset slightly and carried in the centre an almost rectangular 'TR6' badge in vitreous enamel. A horizontal channel-section bar divided the middle of the grille, matt black tape within the channel giving the appearance of a pair of thin horizontal bars. CR/CF series cars received additional stainless steel beading at the top and bottom, in my view somewhat spoiling the appearance.

Badges on the TR4 were largely carried over from the TR3A. The familiar blue and white front medallion, bearing the legend 'TR4', was fitted in the centre of the bonnet about 6in back from the leading edge. The medallion did not carry the manufacturer's name, because in front of this were individual letters forming the word 'TRIUMPH', as used on later TR3As. These same letters were used on the boot lid, fitted into pre-drilled holes at the point where the boot lid turned downwards. The letters were of the 'smooth' polished chromed type, rather than the earlier ribbed type. The only other badge was a new chrome-on-Mazak 'TR4' in script, fitted towards the bottom right corner of the boot lid. The earliest TR4s were, for some reason, built without this boot 'TR4' badge.

TR4As continued to use the Triumph lettering

The TR4 bonnet badge (blue car), a 'shield' medallion with blue and white enamel, was carried over from the TR3A/3B. Unlike the TR2/3, the maker's name did not appear on the badge because it was displayed in separate chromed letters – of the solid, slightly dished type – fixed to the bonnet. These letters continued on the TR4A (white car), but the medallion was replaced by a round badge, unique to the TR4A, based on Triumph's long-established 'Globe of the World' motif. 'Triumph' letters, similar in style to those used at the front, were added in this position to the tail (red car) of all TR4/4As.

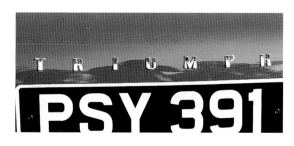

All TR4s except the first few hundred carried an appropriate badge on the right-hand side of the boot lid. For TR4As, except US versions with a live rear axle, an 'IRS' (Independent Rear Suspension) badge went with the updated 'TR4A' motif. Two types of 'IRS' badge were used, the difference being in the bar linking the letters; the bar could be thick (as here) or thin.

The bonnet badge was offset for the TR5 and TR250. Shape and colour were the same for both models, but the badge was used either way up to suit '5' or '250' numbering. The word 'Triumph' did not appear on the front of any of the six-cylinder models.

front and rear, but the medallion was finally consigned to history and replaced by a round plastic badge with a chromed Mazak surround depicting an updated version of the old Triumph 'globe' motif. At the rear, the script badge had the letter 'A' added, and – so that the neighbours could be in no doubt – 'IRS' was also added (but not, of course, on the North American solid axle TR4As). A minor point is that there were two types of 'IRS' badge, the difference being in the thickness of the bar linking the three letters. It was common practice at the time for manufacturers to assist one-upmanship among owners by adding an 'overdrive' badge on cars so equipped, but although Triumph did this on TR5/250s and on some of its other models, it seems that it was never added officially to TR4/4As. The cases reported of such badges being fitted must have been where they were after-market added items.

The TR5 brought further badge updating, the 'TRIUMPH' lettering now disappearing. At the front, the only badge was a beige/cream enamelled motif, with an inverted trapezium shape, carrying 'TR5' in chrome and having a polished edge. In a somewhat eccentric touch, this badge was fitted off the centre line of the bonnet, to the right as viewed from the front – but this did add character to the car! A company press release at the time stated that this repositioning was to make the car look more massive and wide! At the side, on the rear wings just above the marker lights, were plastic rectangular badges stating '2500' in black lettering on a polished background. At the rear, on the right-hand side of the boot lid, the TR5 carried the maker's name in chromed lettering on a beige/cream rectangular badge surrounded with a polished edge. When overdrive was fitted, a further badge announcing this fact was added, and below this was yet another badge, a beige/cream and chromed item reading 'TR5PI'. The 'PI' letters, standing for petrol injection, were in cream on a dark background, presumably to emphasise this feature – big news in 1967!

The TR250 also had unique badging. The bonnet badge, the same shape and colour as the TR5's, read 'TR250'; it was fitted the other way up from the TR5 badge. The rear bore the same

TR5 and TR250 boot badges shared the same colouring, but the injected model announced its special feature with the letters 'PI' (Petrol Injection) on a segment with a dark background. No previous TR had carried an 'overdrive' badge, and to see one on a TR250 is quite unusual – this option was relatively expensive in the US.

The TR5 announced its engine capacity on its rear flanks. The equivalent badge on US cars was of similar style but read 'TR250'. Red side marker lights were fitted for all markets, even where not required by law.

Although the grille badge appeared to be the same on all TR6s, the rendering of 'TR6' changed from vitreous enamel (upper right) to a cheaper decal (lower right) with the introduction of the CR/CF series cars. The difference is subtle, but the characters on the decal version have a slightly crisper outline.

The 'Triumph' name was always announced on the tail of TR6s, but in different styles. Non-US models boasted their use of fuel injection throughout production (upper right), and at first the US carburettor TR6s used a 'Triumph' badge of similar style (centre right). When bumper height was raised for 1975 US models, the maker's badge moved to a plinth in the centre of the bumper (lower right).

'Triumph' badge as the TR5, and below it the designation 'TR250' on a badge equivalent to the 'TR5PI' one, only this was entirely cream/beige with chromed lettering, with no dark shading. The 'overdrive' badge again appeared if applicable. On the rear wings, instead of '2500', the North American car carried plastic 'TR250' badges, which were not quite the same as the TR250 badge at the rear, which was enamel. No 'IRS' badges were fitted to either the TR5 or the TR250.

A further unique feature of the TR250 was the bonnet striping. This ran laterally across the nose to the rear of the bonnet badge, and continued on each side down the front wing to the wheel arch opening. Much controversy has always surrounded this striping, which consisted of a broad central band flanked by a parallel thinner band on each side of the broad stripe. Photographs exist of TR250s on the Coventry production line sporting this stripe, but contrary evidence also exists implying that the stripes were added in the US by dealers. There is also the question of whether the stripes were originally an applied decal, or merely paint-sprayed via a mask or in some other way. A service instruction sheet was reputedly issued showing the exact dimensions and positioning of the stripe so that this could be reproduced, suggesting that it was painted on. Certainly most examples of striping that appear today seem to have been executed in a reflective silvery-blue paint, rather than to have been an applied decal or transfer. The TR250 publicity material stated that the stripes were added to 'emphasise the masculinity theme and the bold look of the car'!

The position regarding TR6 badging is somewhat complex, and is best clarified in model year form as follows:

1969 model year Vitreous enamel 'TR6' medallion on the front grille, part number 717060. 'TR6' decals on rear wings: black for yellow cars, red for white cars, white for all other cars. 'Triumph' name plate badge on rear panel, in black with polished lettering. Below this was a chromed badge reading 'Injection' (except on North American cars). A badge announcing 'Overdrive' was fitted to North American cars if this option was specified, but it seems never to have been used on injection cars.

1970 model year As 1969, plus 'TR6' medallions on the wheel centres.

1971 model year As 1970, although the part number of the enamel front medallion changed to 725400.

1972 model year As 1971, but British Leyland corporate 'plug hole' badges were fitted to the base

The two types of TR6 rear wing decal. Use of the 'Union Flag' version was confined to North American TR6s from the 1973 model year.

of each front wing (from CP/CC 75000). Possibly a few of the last 1971 model year cars also had these badges from new.

1973 model year Injection cars were as for 1972. North American cars were also as for 1972 injection cars except that the TR6 decals on the rear wings were changed to incorporate the Union flag as well as 'TR6' lettering.

1974 model year The front grille medallion on all cars was now a decal (part number ZKC 1224) instead of enamelled. The rear 'Triumph' badge remained unchanged in appearance, but its part number altered to 627563.

1975 model year The maker's badge on North American cars, which now had raised bumpers, moved from the right-hand side of the rear panel to a plinth on the centre of the bumper. The style was still silvered lettering on a black background, but the letters were more widely spaced.

1976 model year Badging continued unchanged.

The TR4 carried no other external chromed decoration save that already described, but one must not overlook the stainless steel beading that ran along the edge of all the outer wings, including down the rear of the car under the light units. This beading was used also on the TR4A/5/250 models, but on the six-cylinder cars it was oversprayed in body colour paint. The small amount of beading used on the rear wing tops of 1969 model year TR6s was also painted. This overpainting was probably done to simplify production, but it was also claimed to make the car look wider. A polished, anodised aluminium capping rail finished off the top of the rear of the TR4 cockpit, the soft-top fixings being accommodated in this. On very early TR4s the cockpit cappings were of chromed brass rather than aluminium.

The TR4A had a stainless steel finishing strip running from a point on the door just above the handle to meet the chromed side light and indicator repeater unit on the front wing. This same type of strip was used on the TR5/250, although

it was slightly wider. The TR5/250 also had a narrow stainless steel trim strip running between the front and rear wheel arches, on the outer edge of the sill just below the door. CP/CC series TR6s shared this narrow sill trim, which was widened for the CR/CF series cars, but TR6s lacked the trim section between the door and front wing. The sills on TR5/250s were painted black, irrespective of body colour, up to the level of the stainless steel trim, apparently to make the car appear lower. It seems, however, that the equivalent area of rear wing below the wrap-around bumper sides was left body colour. All TR6s also featured matt black sills.

The TR5/250 was the first TR to be given an external mirror as standard, a single satin-chromed one being mounted on the driver's door. A matching one for the passenger side could be added as an accessory; this was in fact the same mirror, as it was designed to be assembled to suit either side. The TR6 reverted to the earlier practice of not having an external mirror as standard, but owners frequently fitted them. The TR5 type mirror (part number 622352) was available to special order on TR6s up to 1973, but subsequently more modern door mirrors were offered. For home market cars a variety of British Leyland 'corporate' mirrors were available for dealer fitment, whereas North American cars were listed as having 'Bullet' style mirrors on both sides as standard – but again these may have been fitted by dealers rather than the factory.

Windscreens were basically similar throughout the series. The pressed steel frame had at each bottom corner a peg which engaged in a hidden socket and bracket arrangement mounted within the scuttle top area, the peg having a securing nut at its base. There were also three fixing bolts across the top of the dashboard. All these cars, therefore, had removable windscreens, although rust and lack of use of the facility over the years can make you doubt the fact. The same complete windscreen assembly part number was listed for TR4As through to TR6s, but the TR4 assembly had different top rail fixings for the soft-top. From TR4 body number 24576 CT, the windscreen seal finisher became a one-piece item. TR4s and TR4As

'Corporate image' disease afflicted the TR6 towards the end of 1971, when the British Leyland 'plug-hole' badge appeared low down on both front wings.

had only a rubber seal at the windscreen frame base, but the later cars had an additional internal black plastic finishing strip at this point. They also had matt black side finishers at either side of the windscreen, and along the top horizontal internal part of the windscreen assembly. The windscreen glass itself was retained by a rubber seal with an inserted chromed or satin finish moulding. The windscreen head rail changed with the advent of the TR5/250.

Windscreen glass is a matter of some debate, as there are conflicting details in various pieces of factory literature. The TR4 was said to have had laminated glass as standard upon its introduction, but in other literature this was said to have been optional, toughened glass being the standard offering. In practice, it seems that many TR4/4As did have laminated glass fitted (and charged for) whether or not it had been specifically ordered. In the case of TR250s, laminated glass was not mentioned in the brochure as being available as an option, nor was it said to be fitted as standard. It appears that TR250s mostly had toughened glass screens, which also appeared on TR5s, although in the case of the TR5 the laminated screen was definitely offered as an option. On TR6s, 'Zebra-zone' zone-toughened screens seem to have been the most common fitting, having been phased in to replace the earlier type of toughened screen from early 1970. A laminated screen remained an option, although the build records show that surprisingly few cars were fitted with one. Screen frames on TR4/4A/5/250 models were finished in body colour, but TR6 frames were matt black – with the exception of 1969 model year cars (up to CP 50001) which also had body colour frames. The frame on TR4/4A/5/250s was fitted with two extra clips if the Surrey top was supplied from the factory. The polished aluminium top capping rail on cars built new with 'Surrey' tops also differed from that supplied with roadsters.

On CR/CF series TR6s the hinged ventilation flap forward of the windscreen on the earlier cars was dropped in favour of a permanently fixed plastic air entry grille supplying fresh air to the car and to the heater unit. Although there was no longer any need, now that the hinged flap had gone, for the right-hand wiper arm to be cranked, it nevertheless remained so until the end of production. Details about windscreen wiper blades are given on page 63.

Three very different types of hard-top existed. Introduced with the TR4 was the then unique 'Surrey' top, later reinvented by several continental manufacturers as the 'Targa' top. A cast aluminium rear frame incorporating a wrap-around rear window was semi-permanently bolted to the car and gave as an ancillary benefit some measure of roll-over protection. Between the rear window frame and the windscreen frame one normally had a steel roof section (although those on early TR4s were made in aluminium), this having two fixing bolts each at front and rear to fix it to the screen and rear frame, forming a secure hard-top. As the centre section was too big to be carried in the car when removed, a temporary centre cover of soft-top material was available to fill the gap. This was the piece that was correctly referred to as the 'Surrey' top. This stretched over a light-weight folding framework that pegged and clipped into the windscreen top and the rear screen surround. The whole arrangement was most ingenious and worked well, its only disadvantage being its expense. It could be ordered new with the car, or fitted as an after-market conversion. Cars built with 'Surrey' tops were not normally supplied with soft-tops or soft-top frames. When supplied with a new car, the 'Surrey' top was normally finished in body colour, although contrasting colours (usually black or white) could be ordered. The 'Surrey' top was also available for TR4As and TR5s but differed slightly in the type of fixing bolts and spacers used. TR5 hard-tops had fixing bolts in either chrome or 'blackadized'

The right-hand wiper had to be cranked to clear the hinged ventilation flap when in the open position (right). Even after the flap had been replaced by a black plastic intake grille (far right), for the later CR/CF series TR6s, the crank remained! At the same time the bright finish (satin or chrome) for wipers and arms changed to matt black.

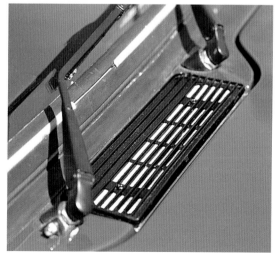

The versatile 'Surrey' top arrangement, seen on a TR250 (top) with centre section removed and on a TR5 (above) with metal roof panel in place. In both cases the rear window surround matches body colour, but it could also be black or white. It is fairly unusual to see a 'Surrey' top on a TR250, as a one-piece glass-fibre hard-top, which was considerably cheaper, was also available for this model. The 'Surrey' soft centre section in position (below) to provide temporary protection. Although the term 'Surrey' top is now used to mean the entire hard-top unit, it was originally meant to refer only to this soft centre section, which was fitted over a lightweight framework and secured by press studs. The windscreen capping rail (below) for a car with a 'Surrey' top contained two large holes for the locating bolts of the centre section.

finish (a factory name for matt black). One minor problem with the 'Surrey' top occurred with owners who arrived home after a pleasant summer evening's drive with the metal centre section removed, and then simply laid it in place to weather-proof the car overnight. They drove off next day forgetting to fasten the bolts, only to see the centre section sail away as soon as 20mph was reached – a large lorry was usually following!

The 'Surrey' top was also available for the TR250, but the brochures for that car do not appear to have promoted it. Nevertheless, factory build records prove that it was supplied on some TR250s from new. The TR250 had the option also of a unique glass-fibre one-piece hard-top never available outside North America. I suspect that this was significantly cheaper than the 'Surrey' top, and was offered as the company was endeavouring to keep North American prices as low as possible – the motive behind the solid-axle TR4A. The glass-fibre top was said to be fully insulated and lined, and to be easily detachable. Its lack of rear quarter windows, however, must have created substantial blind spots.

The TR6 had a completely different one-piece hard-top more suited to the car's angular lines. Again, this could be ordered with the car or fitted later, in matching (usual) or contrasting (rare) colours. This all-steel hard-top was fully trimmed and had fixed rear quarter windows positioned for maximum all-round visibility. Since it was bolted firmly in place, it added considerably to the rigidity of the car (like the 'Surrey' top), as well as rendering it potentially more weather-proof – and thief-proof.

Kits to convert hardtop TR6s into roadsters (and *vice versa*) were available. Cars supplied new with the factory hard-top usually came with no soft-top or other weather equipment, and they also usually had continuous sealing trim at the rear of the doors and side windows.

DIMENSIONS

TR4/4A

Length	12ft 11½in	3.96m
Width	4ft 9½in	1.46m
Height (soft-top up)	4ft 2in	1.27m
Wheelbase	7ft 4in	2.23m
Dry weight	2128lb	970kg
Kerb weight	2240lb	1015kg

TR5 (exceptions to above)

Dry weight	2152lb	981kg
Kerb weight	2268lb	1034kg

TR6 PI

Length	13ft 3in	4.04m
Width	4ft 10in	1.47m
Height (soft-top up)	4ft 2in	1.27m
Wheelbase	7ft 4in	2.23m
Dry weight	2290lb	1041kg
Kerb weight	2408lb	1085kg

TR6 carburettor (exceptions to above)

Length (1973/4 cars)	13ft 6in	4.12m
Length (1975/6 cars)	13ft 7in	4.16m
Kerb weight	2470lb	1120kg

Notes Cars fitted with wire wheels were wider by 2½in. TR4A models with IRS differed slightly from the dry and kerb weights given for the TR4. The TR250 was approximately 30lb lighter than the TR5. Kerb weights for the TR6 carburettor cars depended upon export specification, the figure given being the maximum weight which applied to the final cars.

The one-piece steel hard-top available for the TR6 had very attractive lines and a generous glass area. When supplied with a new car, it almost invariably matched the body colour.

Colour Schemes

Colour and trim combinations were complex and varied. From TR4 number CT 28807, built on 3 January 1964, the different paint colours were each given a two- or three-digit code number which appeared on the car's commission number plate, the numbering being extended as new colours arrived. Also on the plate was a separate two-digit number indicating the trim colour. This colour numbering system continued through to the end of TR6 production.

The colour numbers used on the TR4-6 range are given in the first panel. Note that some colours are paint only, some are trim only and some are both paint and trim. The last number of a code indicates which basic colour group it belongs to: for example, all ending in a '6' are blues and all with a '4' are yellows (Shadow Blue is an exception). Those few colours used on TR4s prior to 1964 and deleted by that date do not have a number – Spa White, Powder Blue, pre-1964 British Racing Green and Velasquez Cream.

It is believed that TR6 PI and carburettor cars shared the same colour ranges while both types were produced simultaneously. Following the demise of the injected car in February 1975, however, carburettor cars appeared in several new colours never available on fuel injected cars.

I have not attempted to give paint manufacturers' references for TR4-6 series colours because matching paints are readily available from commercial sources and, in any event, paint codes tend to go out of date on a regular basis. Full details of paint, trim and soft-top colour combinations for each model are given in the tables.

Triumph used a light blue (below left) to good effect on the TR3A and continued this on the TR4, this shade being known as Powder Blue. Later TR4/4A models and a few TR5s also appeared in a similar blue, although it was called Wedgwood Blue, the change taking place in March 1963.

COLOUR CODES

11	Black	64	Mimosa Yellow
12	Matador Red	65	Emerald Green
13	Light Tan	66	Valencia Blue
16	Midnight Blue	72	Pimento Red
17	Damson	73	Maple
19	New White	74	Beige
23	Siena Brown	75	British Racing Green (1975)
25	Triumph Racing Green (Conifer)	82	Carmine Red
		84	Topaz Yellow
26	Wedgwood Blue	85	Java Green
27	Shadow Blue	92	Magenta
32	Signal Red	93	Russet Brown
33	New Tan	94	Inca Yellow
34	Jasmine Yellow	96	Sapphire Blue
54	Saffron Yellow	106	Mallard Blue
55	Laurel Green	126	French Blue
56	Royal Blue	136	Delft Blue
63	Chestnut	146	Tahiti Blue

TRIUMPH TR4 COLOURS

Paint	Trim
Spa White[1]	Black, Red[8]
Powder Blue[2]	Midnight Blue[9], Black
British Racing Green[3]	Black, Red[8]
Black	Black, (Matador) Red[8]
Signal Red	Black, (Matador) Red[8]
Velasquez Cream[4]	Black, Red[8]
New White[5]	Black, (Matador) Red[8]
Wedgwood Blue[6]	Midnight Blue[9]
Triumph Racing Green[7]	Black

Footnotes
[1] Spa White was available only up to CT 21495, in March 1963. [2] Powder Blue was available only up to CT 20916, in March 1963. [3] British Racing Green was available only up to CT 19518, in January 1963. [4] Velasquez Cream was found only on a small number of cars in 1961. [5] New White was available only from CT 21520, in March 1963. [6] Wedgwood Blue was available only from CT 21247, in March 1963. It was a slightly darker shade than the former Powder Blue. [7] Triumph Racing Green (also called Conifer Green) was available only from CT 19521, in January 1963. Triumph Racing Green is not the same colour as the previous British Racing Green. It is possible that Matador Red trim was available with Triumph Racing Green in addition to Black, but no specific confirmation has yet been found. [8] It is uncertain whether Red trim was Matador Red from the start of production, or whether the Red trim colour was changed. An American sales brochure dated October 1961 indicates that Spa White was also available with Blue trim in addition to Red and Black. [9] It is uncertain whether Blue trim was Midnight Blue from the start of production, or whether the Blue trim colour was changed.

General notes
Soft-tops were available in black or white for all colour schemes, with the possible exception of Velasquez Cream, for which only black may have been offered; tonneau covers usually matched soft-top colour. 'Surrey' soft-tops were only available in black or white. Hard-tops could be specified in black, white or body colour. Trim could be in Vynide or leather; if in leather, the trim code number on 1964-65 cars was prefixed 'H' on the commission plate, prior to the colour number. The windscreen frame was stated to be painted to match the hard-top on all cars supplied new with one, but whether this always happened in practice is uncertain.

Signal Red ran from the TR2 of 1954 to the 1970/71 TR6s, longer than any other TR colour, even Black. Strong sunlight sets off the vivid hue on this TR4 – a real sports car red!

Several shades of white appeared over the years, this one, correct for a TR4A, being New White. This replaced Spa White in March 1963 and ran right to the end of TR6 production in 1976.

TRIUMPH TR4A COLOURS

Paint	Trim
Black	Black, Matador Red
New White	Black, Matador Red
Triumph Racing Green	Black, possibly Matador Red
Wedgwood Blue	Midnight Blue
Signal Red	Black, Matador Red
Royal Blue[1]	Black, Midnight Blue
Valencia Blue[2]	Black, Light Tan

Footnotes
[1] Royal Blue was a new colour, believed introduced in March 1966 from approximately CTC 67685. [2] Valencia Blue, principally a TR5/250 colour, was used on some late TR4As, probably only in the last three months.

General notes
Soft-tops were available in black or white for all colour schemes; tonneau covers always matched soft-top colour. 'Surrey' soft-tops were available in black or white. Hard tops could be specified in black, white or body colour. Trim could be Ambla or leather; if in leather, an 'H' prefix appeared before the trim colour number on the commission plate. The note to the TR4 table concerning windscreen frames applies also to TR4As.

TRIUMPH TR5/250 COLOURS

Paint	Trim
New White	Black, Matador Red
Triumph Racing Green	Black, Light Tan
Signal Red	Black
Jasmine Yellow	Black, Light Tan
Royal Blue	Black, Shadow Blue[1]
Valencia Blue	Black, Light Tan
Black[2]	Matador Red, possibly Black
Wedgwood Blue[3]	Black, Midnight Blue

Footnotes
[1] Midnight Blue trim may have been used on some Royal Blue cars. [2] Black was definitely available on the TR250 and probably also on the TR5, although it was very rare. [3] Wedgwood Blue, although not apparently a catalogued colour for these cars, was certainly used on a few TR5s and TR250s.

General notes
TR5 and TR250 models are believed to have shared the same colour range; the colour of the TR250's nose stripes is described in the 'Body & Exterior Trim' section (page 29). Soft-tops were now predominantly black, but some cars with white soft-tops have been found in factory records; white *may* have been available with all colour schemes. Tonneau covers always matched soft-top colour. Hard-tops could be specified in black, white or body colour. Trim was almost always in Ambla; leather was now very rare on TR5s, if indeed it was actually available at all. Although leather was mentioned in Standard-Triumph literature, TR Register experts have never actually seen a car originally specified with it. However, a few TR250s were supplied with leather trim.

TRIUMPH TR6 COLOURS (CC/CP series, by model year)

Paint	Trim 1969	Trim 1970	Trim 1971	Trim 1972
Damson	Black, Light Tan	Black, New Tan[1]	Black, New Tan	Black, Grey, New Tan
New White	Black, Matador Red, Light Tan	Black, Matador Red, New Tan[1]	Black, Matador Red, New Tan	Black, New Tan, Shadow Blue[2]
Triumph Racing Green[3]	Black, Light Tan, Matador Red?			
Signal Red	Black, Light Tan	Black, New Tan[1]	Black, New Tan	
Jasmine Yellow	Black, Light Tan	Black, New Tan[1]		
Royal Blue[4]	Black, Shadow Blue	Black, Shadow Blue	Black, Shadow Blue	
Siena Brown		Black, New Tan[5]	Black, New Tan	New Tan
Laurel Green		Black, New Tan[1], Matador Red?	Black, New Tan[6]	Black
Saffron Yellow			Black, New Tan	Black
Sapphire Blue[4]			Black, Shadow Blue	Black, Grey, Shadow Blue
Pimento Red				Black
Emerald Green				Black, Grey

Footnotes
[1] New Tan replaced Light Tan early in 1970, so earlier cars in 1970 model year would instead have had Light Tan. [2] Shadow Blue trim might have been offered for New White cars before the 1972 model year. [3] Triumph Racing Green was often referred to as Conifer Green in various factory publications. These two colours are the same. [4] Royal Blue appears to have been replaced by Sapphire Blue early in 1971, so both colours were used in the 1971 model year. [5] Siena Brown appears to have been introduced early in 1970, so may never have been found with Light Tan trim. [6] New Tan trim may have been offered for Laurel Green cars into the 1972 model year.

General notes
Soft-tops and tonneau covers (if fitted) were normally black, but white was found on a few early cars in the 1969 model year and was available to special order thereafter. It is believed that hard-tops supplied with new TR6s almost always matched the body colour, although it is thought that contrasting colours may have been available to special order up to the 1972 model year. Pimento was sometimes spelled 'Pimiento' in factory publications.

A particularly attractive and unusual shade was Valencia Blue, used only on a few very late TR4As, plus the TR5/250, perhaps for 18 months in total. This colour combined with the TR250 silver stripe looks particularly striking.

Damson, used on TR6s for
the 1969-72 model years,
was fairly popular when
the cars were new but is
not often seen now. This
is a pity as it gives the
TR6 a majestic look,
especially in combination
with the matching hard-
top. Laurel Green was an
attractive TR6 colour that
took the place of Triumph
Racing Green for the
1970 model year,
continuing for several
seasons until a later
Racing Green arrived.
Sapphire Blue particularly
suits the TR6. This rich
colour perfectly
complements the
handsome and purposeful
shape of the Karmann-
bodied TR.

TRIUMPH TR6 COLOURS (CF/CR series, by model year)

Paint	Trim 1973	Trim 1974	Trim 1975	Trim 1976	Trim 1976[1]
New White	Black, Chestnut, Shadow Blue	Black, Chestnut, Shadow Blue	Black, Chestnut, Shadow Blue	Black, Chestnut	Black, Beige
Siena Brown	Black, New Tan				
Mimosa Yellow	Black, Chestnut	Black, Chestnut	Black, Chestnut	Black, Chestnut, Beige	Black, Chestnut, Beige
Emerald Green	Black	Black			
Pimento Red	Black, Chestnut	Black, Chestnut	Black, Chestnut	Black, Chestnut	Black
Carmine Red	Black, New Tan	Black, New Tan	Black	Beige	Beige
Magenta	Black	Black			
Sapphire Blue	Black, Shadow Blue	Black, Shadow Blue			
Mallard Blue	Black, New Tan	Black, New Tan			
French Blue	Black	Black	Black	Black	Black
Maple		Black, New Tan	Black	Beige	Beige
British Racing Green (1975)				Black, Beige	Beige
Topaz Yellow[2]				Black, Beige	Black, Beige
Java Green				Black	Black
Delft Blue				Black, Beige	Black, Beige
Russet Brown					Beige
Inca Yellow					Black
Tahiti Blue					Black, Beige

Footnotes

[1] The last column indicates colours in use towards the end of production in July 1976; CF (North American carburettor) models had an altered range in the last few months. Of these colours, Russet Brown, Inca Yellow and Tahiti Blue were also used on MGBs and MG Midgets. However, Mallard Blue is *not* the same colour as MG's Green Mallard, nor does it appear that the TR6's British Racing Green matches any similar MG or BMC/BL colours. The TR6's Carmine Red *may* be the same as MG's Carmine Red. [2] Topaz was not listed as available for 1975 injection TR6s, but it was in fact available during the last few months of the injected car's run, and one or two original examples are known.

General notes

The trim colours listed may not be exhaustive. Carpet colours matched trim, except New Tan carpet was supplied with Chestnut and Beige trim. Soft-tops and tonneau covers were probably always in black, but white would have been possible as a special order. Hard-tops were always body colour from the 1973 model year onwards.

Pimento Red ran from the 1972 model year to the end of production, this particular car being a 1973 TR6 that has been in the same ownership almost from new, and still wears its original paint. The soft-top, which is also original, is unusual in being white rather than the more common black.

Interior Trim

For just over the first year of TR4 production, the model was provided with TR3A type seats, identical in all important respects to those of the earlier model. With these seats, which were of the 'bucket' type, the upholstery 'panelling' of the cushion and backrest ran transversely across the central portion. The front part of the cushion and the top part of the backrest were plain, divided from the panelled portion by piping, which was also used on the extremities of the seats. Piping could be either contrasting (usually white) or of the same colour as the seat itself. The back of the seat backrest was a single plain panel.

The cushions were located in the seat pan solely by gravity, and the passenger seat was arranged so that the backrest could be tipped forward for access to the rear of the cockpit. Springs and horsehair were used for stuffing both cushion and backrest. The seats were upholstered in Vynide or optional leather. If leather was spec-

ified, only the seats, and no other item of trim, were in leather, and even the rear of the backrests remained in Vynide and the piping in plastic. From late TR4s onwards, cars with leather trim had a letter 'H' added to the trim colour number on their commission plates. Both seats were adjustable on floor-mounted sliding runners (made by the Leveroll company), painted grey or silver.

A completely new design of TR4 seat was substituted around the end of 1962, at body number CT 15076. Now the whole seat tipped forward for access to the rear, whereas with the earlier design only the backrest tipped. From body number CT 20925 both seats were made to tip forward. The new seats had flatter, wider seat cushions, and backrests that were more right-angled in section at the top. Pleating was now longitudinal and extended over the whole cushion and backrest. The seat frames were entirely new, and the seats were now filled with foam rubber over a rubber

Seats in the early TR4 were carried over virtually unchanged from the TR3A/3B. Contrasting piping was common on all TR4/4A/5/250 models. Note the seat slide adjustment lever at the front corner of the nearer seat. A correct steering wheel is also seen.

The later style of TR4 seat, unique to TR4s built after body number 15076 CT, featured a squarer cushion, thicker backrests with less curvature, and different pleating. The wood-rim steering wheel is not original.

stretcher plate, rather than the old 'springs and horsehair' system. All seats had piping, frequently in white but also quite commonly the same colour as the upholstery.

Seats on the TR4A remained similar in overall shape, but were now more heavily padded and upholstered in ICI's then new Ambla – this gave

rise to the slogan 'the seat that breathes'! – that had replaced Vynide generally as a trim material in the mid-'60s. Leather seats continued to be an option. Whereas the later TR4 longitudinal seat pleating covered the whole cushion and backrest facings, the TR4A seat had pleating only in the centre sections, a padded rolled edge being incorporated in addition. The piping on the top of the TR4A backrests also continued further towards the rear of the seat top, which had a less angular contour than the late TR4 type. In the TR4A (and the TR5/250) the seat runners were slightly repositioned and canted outwards towards the front, both to give the illusion of more space and more particularly to make the seat clear the gearbox tunnel when fully forward or tipped. As on the late TR4s, both seats tipped on the TR4A/5/250s.

TR5/250s had unique seats, described as upholstered in 'embossed Ambla'. Leather was still an option but was now very rarely specified, presumably because customers found Ambla more satisfactory than Vynide. Although specific to the TR5/250, the seats were only altered in detail from the TR4A type. The pleated sections now contained numerous 'breathing holes' and the pleats ran right to the front of the cushions. Road testers commented on their greater comfort and thigh support, but these seats were still non-

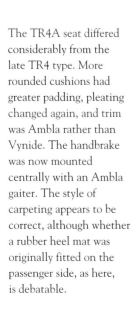

The TR4A seat differed considerably from the late TR4 type. More rounded cushions had greater padding, pleating changed again, and trim was Ambla rather than Vynide. The handbrake was now mounted centrally with an Ambla gaiter. The style of carpeting appears to be correct, although whether a rubber heel mat was originally fitted on the passenger side, as here, is debatable.

TR5/250 seats were finished in 'Embossed Breathing Ambla' (above), as seen on a TR5. There were perforations in the cushions and pleats that went right to the front of the seat. TR250 interior (above right) shows the very unusual leather trim option for the seats, with no Ambla-style perforations visible.

Two of the numerous TR6 seat designs (below), none of which had contrasting piping. The car with Light Tan trim (left) is from the 1970 model year and shows the 'high-back' style of seat, with built-in but adjustable head restraints, used in various forms for North American CC series cars. The car with Chestnut trim (right), an unusual but correct colour, shows the later CR/CF series seat, which for the North American market always came with head restraints, now of the removable variety.

reclining and no provision for fitting headrests was made, even on TR250s. Catches were now incorporated in the tipping mechanism to ensure that the seats did not pivot under hard braking. Piping was now used only around the edges of the seat; its colour could still be the same or contrasting.

TR6s had a multiplicity of different types of seat. The 1969 model non-US cars had a development of the TR5 seat, but the pleating, still with breathing holes, now ran laterally. Padded rolls were fitted all round the central pleats. This early type of non-US seat still had no reclining mechanism nor headrest provision. US specification 1969 TR6s had a non-reclining seat of largely similar design, but of 'high back' type with built-in headrests fitted as standard. These headrests were arranged to fold forward so as not to interfere with the tonneau cover, which had no headrest pockets. The lateral pleating ran the full height of the seat, including the headrest.

At the start of the 1970 model year, from CP/CC 50001 onwards, a reclining mechanism was at last added for all markets. A chromed operating lever was fitted on the outside of each seat, roughly at the point where the cushion meets the backrest. The black-painted lever that operated the seat release catch was situated at almost the same point. The 'high-back' US seat continued with various modifications, some inspired by US safety legislation which caused frames and runners to be strengthened. However, the headrests no longer folded forwards and as a result pockets were fitted in the tonneau cover. Headrests were still not available, even as options, outside the North American market.

At the end of 1972, when the CR/CF series cars arrived, an attempt was made to commonise the alternative seat types for US and non-US models. The new seats were invested with fire-resistant properties by a change of padding material, which was now fire-retarding foam, but pleating and trim rolls were broadly as before. Seat upholstery, with ventilated facings, now had a

coarser grain, a US sales brochure describing the material as 'expanded PVC leathercloth'. These seats had provision for separate head restraints, which were adjustable and removable, and were trimmed and padded to match the rest of the seat. Tonneau pockets were supplied even though the head restraints were removable. Cars supplied to North America always had head restraints, it is thought for legislative reasons, but for other markets they were optional, although frequently specified. When head restraints were not specified, small blanking plugs were provided for the seat tops. Tonneaux with or without pockets could be supplied for non-US injection TR6s. Both seats continued to be hinged so as to tip forwards, restraining catches being provided. All TR6 seats were piped, but the piping was no longer in contrast to the seat's main colour.

I should add that TR6 seats alone take up almost 60 pages of the 1973 TR6 parts catalogue, taking into account the many export and other variations, so it is regrettably not possible to list all the minutiae of their development here! Some US TR6 seats (from 1974 model year) were even equipped with sensor pads, which activated a buzzer, to ensure that occupants donned their seat belts. As to whether leather trim was available on TR6s, the first three editions of the TR6 parts catalogue (ie, up to the introduction of the CR/CF

From the 1970 model year, TR6s were equipped with reclining seats, operated by the chromed lever seen below. The black lever worked the seat tipping release mechanism. Both seats had release catches, even though no occasional rear seat was available!

The superbly trimmed interior of a concours-winning TR6. The trim colour is Shadow Blue. Correct carpets and seat belts are on show, as is the earlier type of TR6 tunnel-mounted interior light. Even though this is a late CP series car, no head restraints are fitted.

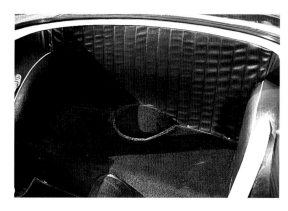

Rear compartments of two early TR4s (above and near right), with and without the optional rear seat. When this seat was not specified, the ledge was carpeted to match the footwells. Visible in the upper view is the way only the backrest of the early TR4 seat tips forward. The built-in mounting point for the static type of seat belt can be seen on the rear wheel arch, but pre-1965 UK cars were not obliged to have the belts actually fitted. The soft-top is stored behind the padded rear cover. When a car was equipped from new with a 'Surrey' top, the pleated rear cover had no padding (bottom right). Rear compartments of TR4/4A/5/250 models were all broadly similar, but by this stage – this is a TR5 – seat belt mountings had moved to the top of the wheel arch. The other view, of a TR250 with 'Surrey' top (top right), shows how the whole seat tipped forwards from late TR4s onwards. Note how Furflex and rubber seals continue right round the door and hard-top edges.

series) list it, but in practice it seems not to have been available. Neither I nor the TR Register's TR6 Registrar has ever seen a car so trimmed as originally supplied.

An occasional rear seat cushion was an optional extra from the start of TR4 production, this being a rectangular seat, with piping and longitudinal pleating, fitting directly on the existing ledge. Whether or not the occasional seat was ordered, vertically pleated lift-up panels were fitted at the rear and sides of the rear compartment on the roadster (as opposed to 'Surrey' top) models; these neatly hid the soft-top and its frame. Cars supplied new with a hard-top had fixed, non-padded panels at this point. The occasional rear seat continued to be listed for the TR4A, but its practicality was reduced because the TR4A's new folding soft-top (see pages 53-54) occupied so much of the rear space when lowered. Although the rear bulkhead trim panel no longer served to conceal the soft-top after the adoption of the folding version, it continued to be used, still with vertical pleating but now without padding, right through to early TR6s. From 1970 model year CP/CC TR6s onwards, it became a plainer design with just two horizontal pleats. The occasional rear seat does not appear to have been available on the TR5, nor on the TR6, even though a TR6 supplied new with a hard-top instead of a soft-top

would have had plenty of room for such a seat to be fitted.

The footwells of early TR4s were covered with rubber mats (with pleated heel sections), which were long enough to cover the lower inner front bulkhead and were secured by press-stud fasteners fixed to the floors. Later TR4s (no exact change point has been found) were given footwell carpets, with a rubber heel mat let into the carpet on the driver's side. On all TR4s (and subsequent models), carpet covered the rear floors, differential cover, transmission tunnel, gearbox cover, front bulkhead sides and rear around the tunnel join, inner wing area in the footwells (where carpet was glued to millboard), B post reinforcement pads, sill edges, and heelboard and rear seat

The rear interior of a TR6, showing the design of back panel used from the 1970 model year. Even on TR6s built new with a hard-top, no occasional rear seat cushion option was offered.

not reach to the top of the doors, the exposed sections being painted body colour. Chromed door fittings comprised cranked window winder handles with black plastic knobs (the design changed slightly at CT 20310), a door pull handle at the top of the door trim, and a door release and locking handle at the front of the door. The rear wheel arches were covered in lightly padded Vynide and piped around the edges.

The same basic trim layout was used on the TR4A and TR5/250, but with slight modifications. TR4As were described in brochures as having 'deep-pile' carpet throughout, but there may have been some poetic licence here. The underfelt now specified for the floor carpets was very much a mixed blessing, for it soaked up water and promoted floor corrosion. Two types of Ambla – 'coarse grain' and 'fine grain' – were used for interior trim (including seats) on TR4As, but it would appear that these grain alternatives only occurred for black Ambla, blue and red always being in coarse grain. Black Ambla of fine grain came in with the TR4A, but at CTC 58000 the grain reverted to coarse for the rest of the TR4A's production run.

At the rear, the trim quarter panels and capping rail changed to suit the TR4A's new soft-top design. As with the seats, Ambla replaced

ledge. The carpets were edge-bound and either studded or glued into place as appropriate. A black rubber boot of circular section surrounded the base of the chromed gear lever and mated with the transmission tunnel carpet.

TR4s had rear quarter panel sections and door trims in millboard covered in Vynide, with piping and unequally spaced horizontal pleats. Door trims, incorporating slim Vynide map pockets, did

Door trim comparison on TR4 (red car) and TR5/250 (blue car). Although the style is similar at a glance, there are detail differences in the door release and window winding handles, the pull handles (chromed on the TR4, moulded into the padded top trim on the TR5/250) and the lock mechanisms.

TR6 door trim comparison on early (green car) and late (red car) models. The top trim rail is black irrespective of trim colour. The later door has an inset pull handle, whereas the earlier one continued with the moulded top rail type used on the TR5/250.

Vynide for other aspects of the trim. The doors were now fully trimmed, a grained black plastic capping rail being added to the top of the door, overlapping the door trim panel. The handbrake was now on the transmission tunnel, and surrounded by an Ambla gaiter let into the carpet; for the TR4 there had been a rubber boot at the base of the handbrake where it passed through the floor. A backwards-facing extension to the dashboard support bracket now formed a small console surrounding the gear lever, and it was into this that the rubber boot, still circular in section on the TR4A but more squared-off on the TR5/250, was fitted. On the TR5/250, the door crash pad/capping rail incorporated a moulding to serve as a pull handle, the chromed handle being deleted, although both the window winder and door release handle were still chromed.

The TR6's interior trim was similar to that of the TR4A and TR5/250, but with certain differences. In the interests of sound deadening, underfelt was now fitted to the transmission tunnel and heelboard/lower rear bulkhead area. 'Fibroceta' insulating padding was fitted under the wheel arch trims, and further trim panels were placed above the gearbox tunnel under the dashboard area. The rubber gear lever surround was replaced by a PVC/Ambla conical gaiter, described in the parts book as a 'gauntlet'. Door trims were still pleated and fitted with map pockets, but the number of pleats was reduced on cars built from late 1970. Door trims up to and including the 1973 model year CR/CF cars continued without a separate pull handle, the moulding in the top rail trim having to suffice, but 1974 model year CR/CF TR6s onwards had a door pull 'pocket' incorporated into the centre of the door lining panel. These cars also incorporated modern style 'safer' internal handles and window winders.

Sun visors were listed as an option on the TR4, but from the TR4A they were provided as standard. Made of white, padded, grained PVC, they were mounted on a three-piece cranked rail fixed at the centre and at both outer ends to the top of the windscreen frame. TR5/250 visors were black instead of white, and of slightly different shape; the passenger's visor now incorporated a vanity mirror and the TR5/250 visors could be swung out at 90° to obscure sun from the side. The fitting arrangements were also altered and became rather more substantial. Sun visors on TR6s were similar to the TR5/250 type, again finished in black.

The interior mirror was suspended from the top screen rail. Two types were fitted to the TR4, both having a matt black stalk and back, but they differed in their black plastic edging surrounds. The earlier mirror had corners cut off at a 45° angle, whereas the later type had right-angled corners. The design probably changed late in the

TR4's run, and the second type of mirror continued for the TR4A. The TR5/250 had a dipping mirror that was collapsible in the event of impact. It was no longer rectangular, being shorter along the top edge than the bottom and having rounded corners, particularly at the top. This same black-finished dipping mirror was used on all 1969 TR6s. For 1970, a different mirror with a wider field of view was provided for hard-top models, but for some reason hard-top TR6s sold in Sweden had to have the TR5-type mirror normally still supplied on soft-top cars. For 1971 and '72, the hard-top mirror was available with two different head assemblies, the soft-top (and Swedish hard-top) one continuing as previously. CF/CR series TR6s received a different type of interior mirror (part number 632095) on both hard-top and soft-top models for all markets except Sweden, which continued to require the old TR5-type mirror.

Safety belt mountings were incorporated from the start of TR4 production in 1961, while at the beginning of 1967 British Standard 'BS AU 1965' came into force in relation to mountings, reference to this being found on the commission plate. Belts were initially fixed by conventional bolts, but 'eyebolt' fixings, where the belt could be unclipped, became available later. Static lap (two-point) or diagonal belts (three-point) were offered as an option on the TR4 and TR4A, but by the end of TR4A production belts were legally required in several markets, including the UK. Belts, therefore, were normally fitted to new cars, but priced and quoted as an extra. This may be because they were usually fitted by dealers rather than the factory.

It was as late as May 1972 when seat belts – static lap and diagonal belts – were finally fitted as standard and included in the list price; inertia reel belts still cost extra. The three-point static belts usually had their mountings on the rear wheel arch, at the base of the B post and either on the side of the transmission tunnel or on the rear floor adjacent to the tunnel. Inertia reel belts usually had the reel box mounted on the vertical face of the rear wheel arch, although considerable variation occurred as these belts were frequently dealer-fitted. The TR250 brochure stated that the car was equipped as standard with 'spring-loaded' belts, so that the belt returned automatically to its holster – this was presumably some form of inertia reel device. Inertia reel belts never superseded the static type (other than as an option) for home market TR6s, but one assumes that inertia reel belts, or a form of them, were standard for late US market TR6s, as the TR250 had spring-loaded belts as far back as 1967. Illustrations in a 1975 US TR6 brochure certainly show three-point inertia reel belts, and the implication from the text is that they were standard.

TR250 seat belt close-up shows that at least some of the standard belts in these cars carried the manufacturer's name.

The early type of sun visor (below), optional on the TR4 but standard for the TR4A, was finished in white PVC with a prominent grain. The design remained similar for the TR5/250 (bottom), but the trim was now black vinyl with a smooth surface, and a vanity mirror was added on the passenger side. Both views show one of the holes in the polished aluminium top rail for bolting the hard-top, but the earlier car also shows the socket into which the soft-top front rail fits.

Instruments & Controls

The TR4 dashboard was a somewhat austere metal pressing, painted white irrespective of body colour. Spa White was used at first but replaced by New White in 1963 at car number CT 21267. At its outer ends the dashboard had the then unique, but now universal, black 'airflow' ventilation grilles, later claimed to be 'reinvented' by Ford! A knurled wheel in each grille controlled and directed air flow. Triumph did not make as much of this innovation in publicity as it might have done. The lockable glovebox had a metal lid in white fitted with a chromed finger-grip escutcheon surrounding the lock. The central section of the dashboard was a trapezium-shaped panel, with an engine-turned polished metal finish on early TR4s (up to body number 4398 CT) but a black 'crackle' painted finish on later

ones. Set in this were the minor instruments and a pull-out ashtray.

Most instruments on the earlier TR4s were carried over from the TR3A and were of Smiths Industries (Jaeger) manufacture, but the ammeter was by Lucas. Initially convex glasses were used for all instruments, but these were replaced by flat glasses from car numbers CT 11307 (left-hand drive) and CT 15053 (right-hand drive). The dashboard itself also changed slightly at this point. All instruments were surrounded by a chromed bezel and seated on a rubber gasket. Black faces with clear white lettering and pointers were used throughout, and illumination was from the rear.

In front of the driver was a 5in speedometer (reading to 120mph or 200kph) on the left and a matching rev counter (red-lined at 5000rpm) on

The TR4 dashboard, painted Spa White, had an engine-turned, polished centre panel in its original form. Instruments, switchgear, steering wheel and gear knob are all correct on this car. 'Airflow' ventilation grilles, each controlled by a knurled wheel, were an advanced feature that Triumph should have promoted more strongly.

The TR4's two main instruments, with warning lights between, are seen in their earlier form, with convex glass.

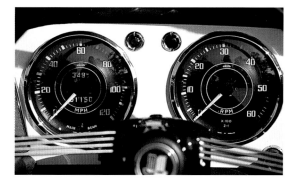

Early TR4 polished centre panel shows correct minor instruments – with fully exposed needles – and switchgear. The temperature gauge is the TR3A capillary type, fitted to a few of the earliest TR4s.

This later TR4 dashboard shows the black crackle finish found on the centre panel of the great majority of TR4s. The wood-rim wheel and wooden gear knob are non-original but common period fittings.

the right. The speedometer contained a trip reading to 999.9 miles, reset by a knurled knob projecting below the instrument. There were several types of speedometer, to take account of differing rear axle ratios and tyre sizes. The number of wheel revolutions per mile was written in small lettering just below the total mileage display. A small red tell-tale for headlight main beam was also incorporated. Between the speedometer and rev counter were set two warning lights (type WL 11), green for indicators and red for ignition. The speedometer was cable driven from the side of the gearbox or overdrive unit, whereas the mechanical rev counter was driven by cable from the distributor drive shaft.

The four subsidiary instruments in the central panel were usually disposed with the temperature gauge bottom left, oil pressure top left, fuel gauge top right and ammeter bottom right, although variations occurred, particularly on North American specification cars. Oil pressure read to 100psi (a metric scale was available) and the ammeter recorded to plus or minus 30 amps. The temperature gauge was marked 0°, 185° and 250° F on 'Imperial' cars, or 30°, 70° and 100° C on 'Metric' ones. This gauge was electrically operated, unlike the TR3A type that was activated by capillary. There is evidence that some, possibly all, of the first few hundred TR4s also had this capillary temperature gauge, marked 185° F at the centre (normal) and 230° F at the 'hot' end. The fuel gauge was marked rather vaguely in quarters but gave a more steady reading than the old TR3A type, having a damper incorporated in the circuit. When flat glasses arrived for the instruments, these four minor gauges ceased to be fully open-faced, the tops of their needles now being shrouded to conceal the pivot points.

The dashboard top, a black-grained plastic moulding with windscreen air vents, was slightly cowled over both the glovebox lid and the main instruments. A semi-padded black-grained moulded rail ran along the bottom of the dashboard, bowing out under the glovebox lid to form a grab handle. In the centre of this rail was a flat switch panel containing the ignition key lock, plus black and silver plastic knobs for the two-stage pull-out light switch, screen wash plunger knob, wiper switch and choke control. Ignition keys were usually from the FP or FS series.

Heater controls, where fitted, consisted of a temperature control which worked the hot water valve on the engine, a single-speed heater blower switch, and a distribution control. These were mounted on the bracing plate/console bracket that anchored the dashboard to the floor via the transmission tunnel. Further details of the changes in this plate will be found in the 'Body & Exterior Trim' section (page 22). Incidentally, the

The TR4A dashboard received polished wood veneer, but the layout was little different from the TR4 and all instruments were carried over. The veneer is unfortunately prone to cracking and discoloration in the sun over the years, as has happened with this exceptionally original car. The switch to the left of the rev counter is not correct. TR4A details show how speedometer and rev counter changed places with left-hand drive. As with later TR4s, minor dials had shrouded needles, and Lucas rather than Jaeger continued to supply the ammeter. Although all instruments are correct, they are a curious mixture of Imperial (speedometer) and metric (oil and temperature gauges), explained by this one-owner car having been bought in Switzerland but later taken to California.

earliest TR4s had the TR3A type brass tap heater valve, soon replaced by a steel item operated by Bowden cable from the dashboard. Above the heater controls was a cut-out, blanked if necessary, for fitting a standard car radio. Panel lighting was rheostat controlled by a rotary switch situated on the dashboard outboard of the steering column. The scuttle ventilator was operated by a cranked lever under the dashboard.

TR4 direction indicators were worked by a steering column stalk, while the optional overdrive was operated by a stalk on the opposite side. These chromed stalks had black plastic finger-grips at their ends. The types of steering wheel are dealt with in the 'Steering' section (page 98). A

moulded black plastic handbrake grip was fitted. Pendant pedals were used, with rubber pads bearing a moulded 'T' for Triumph on the brake and clutch. The bonnet release was a white plastic knob situated below the right-hand side of the dashboard, even on left-hand drive cars.

TR4A instruments were carried over from the later TR4s, and the dashboard layout remained broadly similar. A major change, however, was the use of polished wood veneer for the dashboard, giving a considerable upgrade in quality – so much so that many TR4s have had the TR4A veneer dashboard retrospectively fitted. In fact, the veneered dashboard (part number 903508) was actually available as a special order on left-hand drive TR4s from the autumn of 1964, but no equivalent right-hand drive part was listed. It is possible that the wooden dashboard was even standard on the last few months' production of TR4s for the North American market.

From November 1965, at CTC 62637, the temperature gauge lost its temperature markings and rather vaguely read just 'C' and 'H', for cold and hot. The TR4A rev counter had a red shaded area between 5000-6000rpm, instead of just a red line at 5000rpm; this type of rev counter was also fitted to an uncertain number of later TR4s. The rheostat switch moved to the central switch panel, taking the place vacated by the light switch, which was now a three-position stalk mounted on the steering column and incorporating a headlamp flasher. Indicator and overdrive stalks were on the other side of the column. The wiper switch remained in its previous position, but was now a two-stage pull-out type to control the now standard fitment of two-speed wipers. The

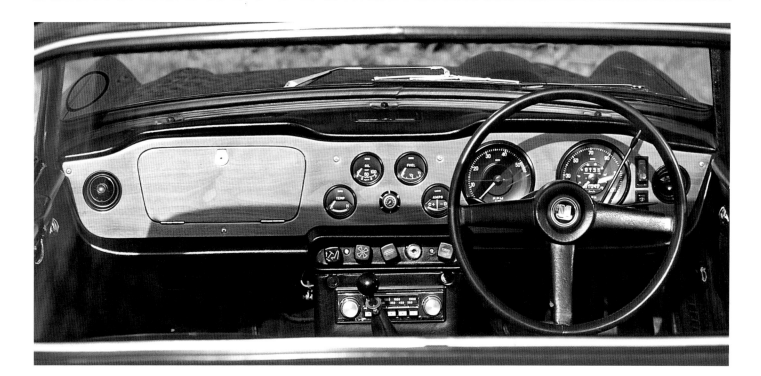

TR5 (and TR250) dashboard retained the same basic style, but the veneer now had a matt finish, all instruments were different, 'eyeball' fresh air vents were introduced, and the ashtray was now inset below the windscreen. Dashboard screws should be matt black. Instrument close-ups for TR5 minor dials and TR250 speedometer and rev counter show the black bezels and different graphics introduced for these cars. Lucas still provided the ammeter, but the other gauges were now marked 'Smiths' instead of 'Jaeger'. Unlike UK TR5s, all TR250s and some export TR5s had tell-tale lamps for brake circuit failure and their standard hazard warning lights, with the switch for these sited below. The red light near the bottom of the speedometer is not original.

The TR5/250 glovebox received an interior light operated by a plunger switch. There was no longer a finger pull on the glovebox lock or a grab handle on the dashboard's lower crash pad.

central console/bracing structure extended backwards to surround the gear lever base and was somewhat padded, a different type of rubber gaiter being required as a result for the base of the lever, which was slightly shortened.

The TR5 and TR250 retained a wooden dashboard of broadly similar layout but in the interests of safety this was now in a non-reflective matt rather than highly polished finish. The glovebox now contained an interior light operated by a trip switch, and there was no longer a finger pull on the lock. The moulded grab handle disappeared, while the ashtray moved to the top of the dashboard, its old position in the centre of the dashboard now occupied by a new design of panel light

rheostat switch in black with a white motif. Panel lighting was now what was called 'variable density blue safety lighting'. The ventilation grilles were deleted in favour of modern swivelling 'eyeball' vents in black plastic. The switch gear was modernised, becoming recessed in the interests of safety, which US legislation was compelling manufacturers to take more seriously.

The same six instrument functions were provided in the TR5 and TR250, but the instruments were of a newer design with matt black bezels, matt black dials and white figures. 'Smiths' rather than the previous 'Jaeger' name now appeared on all except the Lucas ammeter. The temperature gauge was calibrated 'C' and 'H', and the ammeter

'C' and 'D' (for charge and discharge). The rev counter was now shaded yellow between 5000-5500rpm, and red above 5500rpm. The wipers and electric screen washers were controlled by two elongated black 'safety' type rocker switches (made by Clear Hooters Ltd), and the heater fan was now two-speed and controlled from the recessed switch panel. Also on this panel were knobs – now square-headed in black plastic with white motifs – for air distribution, heater temperature and cold start device, and additionally the ignition key. Within the speedometer were two warning lights for main beam and indicators, while the rev counter contained two more for charging and low oil pressure, this latter despite the continued presence of a pressure gauge.

On the TR250, and some left-hand drive TR5s, two additional warning lights were fitted between the speedometer and rev counter. One indicated failure of one of the two split brake pressure circuits and the other indicated operation of the hazard warning lights, the push button for which was sited below the warning lights. The TR250 also had a conventional choke control. If the optional air conditioning system was fitted, a pod with the controls for this was sited in the centre of the dashboard top trim roll. Although the TR250 could hardly be said to need it, both this and the TR5 were now fitted with a speedometer that read to 140mph, although the highest figure marked was 130mph; subsidiary 'kph' markings were also added. At last, the bonnet release knob was moved to the driver's side on the much more numerous left-hand drive cars, this being of course the passenger side on UK specification TR5s. The release knob was now a black 'T-pull' with a white motif.

The dashboard, instrument and control layout for the early TR6 was similar to the TR5/250, with the exception of the steering wheel described in the 'Steering' section (page 98). The ammeter, while looking the same from the front, was changed slightly by having spade terminals in place of the previous screw type. Even an ignition key/starter was still used rather than a steering column lock, although this modern feature finally arrived on the home market in early 1971 at CP 52786. Export specification injection cars and all North American TR6s received a steering column lock somewhat earlier, probably from CC/CP 50001, leading to a minor rearrangement of the switch positions. On 1969 model year cars, the glovebox lock was still polished stainless steel, but from 1970 onwards this was replaced by a matt black version.

Further changes occurred with the introduction of the CF/CR series in late 1972. A facelift was given to the dashboard and controls, principally by reinstating chromed bezels on all the dials and by using updated instrument faces in the style of the Dolomite and Triumph 2000/2.5 range. The maximum figure on the speedometer was now 140mph and the 'kph' markings were more prominent, while the red-lined maximum on the rev counter rose to 5800rpm. The needles on the minor instruments now pivoted from the bottom rather than the top, and the ammeter was deleted in favour of a voltmeter showing battery condition. At last, the antiquated foot-operated dipswitch was replaced by a hand-operated one mounted on the column. In addition, the main headlamp and sidelight switch was moved from the left of the steering column to the right of the dashboard, previously the home of the windscreen

The earlier pattern of TR6 dashboard, entirely correct on this CP series car, was almost identical to the TR5/250 offering. The ignition key space is blank, for a steering lock (just visible) had now become a standard fitting. It is rare to see the original gear knob, as here, since most owners seem to have fitted after-market ones, even on otherwise highly original cars.

Later TR6s of the CF/CR series had a mild facelift for the dashboard, the main change being new instruments with chromed bezels once again. This car, again with the correct steering wheel, is to US specification, as evidenced by some additional switchgear and warning lights.

Late TR6 instruments look very different. Speedometer has more prominent 'kph' markings and 140mph top figure added, while rev counter, now without a yellow segment, is red-lined at a higher 5800rpm. Between these main dials, hazard warning system has a different lamp and switch. Minor dials, now with voltmeter instead of ammeter, have needles that pivot from the bottom. Below them, US cars featured warning lamps for brakes, exhaust gas recirculation and seat belts. Note the period radio.

The pedals from an early left-hand drive TR6, when the foot-operated dipswitch was still fitted. The spring-loaded switch operating the brake lights can be seen at the top of the brake pedal. Pedal rubbers with 'T' motif are correct.

wiper switch, which was now combined with the windscreen washer.

The same matt-finish veneered dashboard continued, and the layout described above remained, with only minor detail alterations, until the end of TR6 production in 1976. North American specification TR6s had written instructions on most of the control knobs rather than the European symbol system, and post-CF1 cars had warning lamps to indicate when various service operations were due, and to advise the driver to don the seat belt. Unlike the TR250, the optional air conditioning controls were fitted under the dashboard on the driver's side, near the air conditioning outlet vent. A similar vent was also fitted on the passenger side.

Weather Equipment

The TR4 used a development of the somewhat outdated 'kit of parts' soft-top found on the TR3A – and on most other '50s sports cars. The soft-top frame, consisting of three transverse bows linked by two bands of webbing, was permanently attached to the interior of the car on each side just behind the top of the door aperture. The soft-top itself, made from vinyl-coated canvas material in black or white with three 'Vybak' windows, was separate from the frame, although provision was made for storage of both items behind lift-up rear and side panels.

The soft-top was attached at the rear by a series of 16 'lift-a-dot' fasteners on the polished aluminium rear tonneau capping rail. Elasticated straps along each side of the soft-top internally helped to keep the material taut above each side window, and the front edge of the soft-top was attached by a three-piece, steel-reinforced, full-

width tongue fitting beneath a lip on the top of the windscreen top rail, making a watertight seal. The outer front edges of the soft-top were fastened to the screen top by a press stud and hook arrangement. Side flaps projected downwards from the soft-top about 1½in further to improve weather sealing at the top of the side window glasses.

Although it took some time and trouble to erect, this soft-top had the advantage that it left the occasional rear seat area available for use, even when the soft-top was folded. This was not the case with the full convertible style soft-top fitted from the TR4A onwards. This later soft-top, permanently fixed to the frame (and thus to the car), was much quicker and more convenient to operate than the earlier type, and the same basic design was used on all post-TR4 cars, with progressive development.

The new 'convertible' soft-top was too large

The TR4 roadster's soft-top erected, showing the tight fit essential for effective weather-proofing. An ample number of 'lift-a-dot' fastenings, 16 of them, featured around the rear.

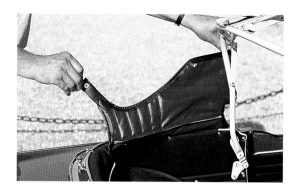

when folded to stow behind the rear panel, so a separate cover was provided, picking up on the rear tonneau fasteners. A black-painted steel transverse angle piece attached the soft-top to the rear deck of the car, and at the front a header rail was attached to the front of the soft-top. Below this was a channel which retained a rubber seal, this clamping down onto the top of the screen frame to provide a watertight joint. Two over-centre toggle catches provided the clamping mechanism. Unlike the previous soft-top, this

These two views show how the rear trim panels lift to allow the TR4 soft-top frame to be neatly folded out of sight. The two types of side panels differ slightly, and that on the red car is thought to be nearer the original pattern, padding being in evidence. 'Tenax' fasteners or press studs were used to hold these panels in place.

The soft-top frame on the TR4 roadster remained permanently fixed to the car, in the same style as the earlier TRs. Correct spacing between the bows was maintained by the webbing supports, which could rot with age, especially if left damp.

The forward end of the TR4 soft-top hooked at each side to the windscreen pillar to ensure that the window sealing strip was taut. This hook arrangement is often omitted on cheaper replacement soft-tops.

The TR4A was the first TR to use the full convertible soft-top, which continued with only minor changes through to the end of TR6 production. The fit above the door glass is not as neat as it might be!

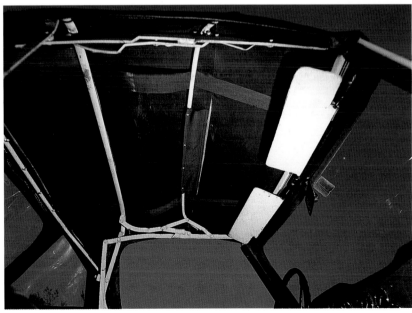

The TR4A soft-top frame still had three transverse bows, but they were linked by a more elaborate mechanism.

A TR5 displays the neat cover available for cars with the convertible style soft-top. The radio aerial is seen fitted in the recommended position.

The soft-top cover came as standard on a TR6, unless a hard-top was specified. Light Tan trim highlights the normal black plastic press studs, known as 'plastic durable dots'! As can be seen, very little usable rear space is left with the top folded. The 'high-back' seats found on earlier US TR6s show well here.

Soft-top contrasts on two UK TR6s. Black was the normal colour, but white was available to special order. The white soft-top is original to this car, proving that the material, if looked after carefully, can easily last a quarter of a century. The black soft-top shows the excellent fit that can be achieved allowing high-speed motoring without flapping or drumming from the material!

An original soft-top on a late TR6, showing the somewhat crudely fitted reflective tape almost invariably used on TR250s and TR6s for the US market.

new type had a positive link by scissors-action metal stays between the front and rear, these running along the top of the glass side windows. Their presence helped both sealing and tension, although the whole arrangement was more complicated and costly. The transverse frame bows were attached to these side supports, although two webbing straps were still used as well. The front bow had a piece of material, which formed part of the soft-top, wound round it as a further location, and straps with press studs were provided at each front corner. A row of external press studs (or sometimes 'lift-a-dot' fasteners) was fitted at the rear of the soft-top to enable the cover to be secured when the soft-top was lowered. The press studs were polished on TR4A/5/250s, and earlier TR6s, but finished in black on later TR6s.

The TR5 had a soft-top which, although similar to the TR4A type, was further refined and improved. The header rail differed, and the catches were now lever types that were turned through 90° to wind the front seal hard down onto the screen frame. These catches were safer, as the levers were arranged so as not to project into the passenger space. Sealing was further improved by the side cant rails having two-piece rubber sections attached to them, these rubbers being

designed to seal to the side window glasses. In addition, Velcro was used to ensure that the soft-top material sealed positively down onto the cant rails. The front corner press studs were deleted.

Contemporary road testers praised the TR5 soft-top as one of the best of its type available, so it is not surprising that the soft-top used for the TR6 was basically identical, with the exception of the addition of a zip-out rear window. The parts manual refers to a special TR6 soft-top 'for German markets only', but I have not been able to establish why this was done. For the TR250 soft-top, strips of silvery reflective tape were sewn and otherwise attached over and to the rear of the car's side windows, and also around the base of the soft-top at the rear. This was stated to be a 'safety feature', but in truth managed to look rather gimmicky and cheap. The reflective tape was variously described as 'white fire' or 'Scotchbrite'. It seems that all TR250s had this feature, and certainly the great majority of American TR6s did as well, although it appears that a few cars did not.

A full tonneau cover was available as an extra from the start of TR4 production but became standard on TR6s in December 1973, except on cars supplied from the factory with a hard-top. Press stud fixings were employed, and on the TR4 special chromed fittings were attached to the dashboard just behind the windscreen, both centrally and towards the edges in front of the air vents. Three press studs were also fitted along the top of each door on TR4As onwards, although these appear to have been omitted on cars sold new with a 'Surrey' top. The tonneau, which had the usual zip set slightly off-centre towards the passenger side, was fixed at the rear by a row of press studs around the rear cockpit finishing rail – but on TR4s it picked up on the 'lift-a-dot' fasteners. The TR5/250/6 had a total of 13 popper press studs around the rear which engaged with the tonneau cover or frame cover, with the further three along each door top and four 'lift-a-dot' fastenings at the front along the dashboard top. The press studs were known officially by the grand-sounding title of 'plastic durable dots'! Tonneaux were made of the same plasticised canvas material used for soft-tops. In addition to the usual pocket for the steering wheel, pockets to accommodate headrests on later cars were included where appropriate, and on some covers a flap was incorporated along either side of the zip fastener to prevent water penetrating through the zip.

A TR6 without a hard-top always had a frame cover supplied as standard. It was only listed as an accessory when it was supplied as part of the hard-top to soft-top conversion kit. The frame cover supplied with this kit differed from the one supplied as standard with soft-top cars in that it had an additional fold and fasteners so that it could fit to the inside of the hard-top when both the hard-top and soft-top were fitted.

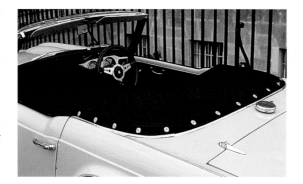

The TR4 tonneau cover, seen in fabric rather than the original Vynide, used the same 16 rear 'lift-a-dot' fixings as the soft-top, plus three press studs at the top of each door.

TR6 tonneau covers on CP series (above) and CF series (left) cars, both with press stud fixings. The UK model shows the central flap arrangement, which helped to prevent water penetrating the zip. With head restraints fitted, as on later US TR6s, suitable pockets were required.

Boot & Tools

Details of the construction and fittings of the boot area will be found in the 'Body & Exterior Trim' section (page 22), but, as for boot trim, the TR4 had very little! At the forward end of the compartment, shielding the petrol tank, was found a millboard panel, painted semi-matt black irrespective of the car's body colour. The sides and outer ends of the boot floor carried no trim at all, although the spare wheel was covered by a plywood (or hardboard) panel which formed the central section of the boot floor and was invariably painted black. At its outer end, the floor panel was secured by two short straps and press studs clipping onto the floor box sections. No boot carpet was fitted. Boot capacity on the TR4-type body was stated to be 5.6cu ft.

The same basic arrangements held good for the TR4A, but the TR5/250, which had wider wheel/tyre combinations, required more vertical space for the spare wheel. Rather than adopt the expensive solution of repressing the boot floorpan panel, a redesigned spare wheel cover panel provided the necessary extra space. The panel now had angle section edges, which served to raise it around 1in above the rest of the floor, giving a rather awkward 'step' profile. Again, the panel was painted black, and still the luxury of carpet had not arrived. Slightly longer straps were used to retain the panel.

The spare wheel itself was held down by a hook and circular plate arrangement, a large wing nut on the hook serving to tighten the wheel against the wheel-well floor, through which a further upwards-facing hook was bolted, attached to the chassis cross tube roughly in its centre. The two hooks engaged to secure the wheel. In the right-hand back corner of the wheel well should be found a strap to retain the wheel-changing tools.

As befitted its move 'upmarket', the TR6 had a lined boot (except at the back), which now sported an interior light under a translucent cover positioned in the front wall of the boot lining. The light was operated automatically by raising the boot lid. Black millboard casing panels formed the boot lining 'box', with cut-outs for the hinges and boot stay. A black carpet was also provided, equipped with neatly-bound edges and held down

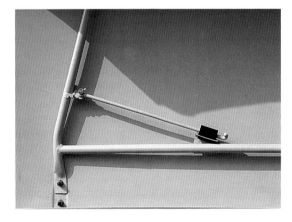

Early TR boot was uncarpeted, the only trim being the front panel. Early type of manual boot prop can be seen in use, and, in the detail view, clipped into the rubber receiving socket on the lid.

by press studs. Under the carpet was still found a removable false floor panel over the spare wheel, but this was now retained by a turn-buckle arrangement. Again, the width of the spare wheel led to the boot floor being slightly raised centrally to cover the wheel, although the fitted carpet disguised this to some extent. As the TR6's boot lid no longer extended down to bumper level, extracting the spare wheel took considerably more effort than with the earlier cars.

The subject of tools is complicated, for it is uncertain what tools were supplied when, and whether a tool kit (other than the basic wheel-changing tools) was always a standard provision. Certainly some TR4/5/6s were supplied without a tool kit, but one can only speculate whether this was factory policy at the time or whether tool kits simply 'went missing' during the chain of delivery of the car to the owner.

Dealing first with the wheel-changing tools, the TR4 had the same jacking arrangement as the sidescreen TRs – a pillar jack that passed through the floor panels just forward of the seats and engaged by means of a hook onto the chassis itself. In theory, this allowed an owner to jack the car from within if the weather was inclement! Only one jacking point was provided each side, the front and rear wheels on the appropriate side both being lifted simultaneously. Large circular rubber plugs blanked the floor holes when not in use. These holes remained in the floors right through to the TR6, despite the fact that a change to a scissors type of jack for the TR4A made them redundant – they must have puzzled some later TR owners as to their purpose!

The TR4 pillar jack was not particularly stable, so many owners chose to use instead a scissors or bottle jack. Indeed, a one-owner TR4 known to me was supplied new in mid-1963 with a bottle jack for placing under the chassis – a much more satisfactory arrangement. This car, the owner confirms, never had a pillar jack. Red seems to have been the most common colour for the pillar jack, although black also appears. The ratchet handle, of two alternative types, was usually red or black to match, or left its natural metal colour. The jack had a non-slip studded foot, and operated by means of an internal screw. Retracted, it was roughly 13in long, and was secured in the boot by a strap.

The scissors jack provided for the TR4A/5/250/6 was a safer and quicker arrangement, *Autocar*'s road testers commenting on the rapidity of wheel-changing on a TR4A with this equipment. It could be easily placed under the appropriate corner of the chassis to lift the desired wheel, rather than having to lift the whole side of the car as had the TR4 pillar jack. The jack could be painted black (most common), green, red or even blue, and was supplied with a matching 'bent wire' handle to operate it.

Any car with disc wheels was supplied in addition with a wheelbrace to loosen the nuts. The earlier type, used up to the TR5/250, was similar to the TR3A style, having a ⅞in AF socket welded to the end of a shaft just over 12in long, with a handle that folded out at right angles to provide sufficient leverage; a spring ensured that the handle clicked into place. The TR6 wheelbrace

was a one-piece tool of conventional right-angled type. Both wheelbraces were normally finished in black. TR4/4As with wire wheels were equipped with a wooden-handled copper hammer (usually of 'Thor' manufacture) for tightening and releasing the knock-off nuts. For the octagonal 'safety caps' found as standard on TR5/250/6s with wire wheels, a special spanner (finished in black) and mallet were provided.

In addition to wheel-changing tools, a TR4

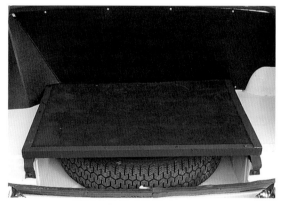

Late TR4 boot received an automatic stay to support the lid. Floor panel has been removed to expose the spare wheel, which wears an authentic Michelin X radial tyre. The wing nut arrangement for securing the wheel is shown.

For the TR5/250, the wheel cover board acquired angle-section edges to make it sit about 1in higher, slightly longer securing straps thus becoming necessary. With the board removed, the reason becomes apparent: wider wheels and tyres were fitted to these cars.

The TR6 boot retained a removable floor for access to the spare wheel, but was now lined with black millboard on the three more visible sides. Note the interior light, which was illuminated automatically by raising the lid.

The TR6 tool kit above remains unaltered from new and includes the later type of one-piece wheel nut spanner. The jack and handle came in various colours. Although neither complete nor accurate, the other tool kit (right) nevertheless shows a representative selection of the items found in TR kits of the period.

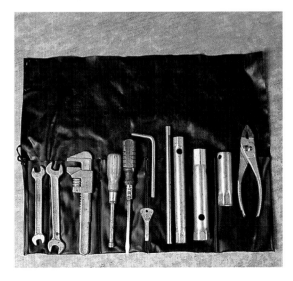

tool kit, if provided, consisted of the following, according to the parts catalogue: headlamp trim removal tool, three open-ended spanners (⅜in × ⁷⁄₁₆in AF, ½in × ⁹⁄₁₆in AF and ⅝in × ¾in AF), tube spanner (½in × 0.56in – an odd combination of measurements that must have had some specific purpose), sparking plug spanner, adjustable spanner, slip joint grips (pliers), screwdriver (bent metal type rather than wooden-handled), tommy bar, grease gun (home and export types, for some

reason), combination tool (used for wheel trim removal, but also able to double as a headlamp trim remover and tommy bar if these items were not present), feeler gauge assembly and a second small screwdriver (this doubled as a 'distributor gauge', presumably to set the points gap). The tools were provided with a tool roll, which came in various materials – vinyl plastic, canvas or canvas-reinforced plastic – and again usually in black, but other colours are seen.

The TR4A tool kit appears to have been the same as the TR4 type, although there will inevitably have been minor differences caused by differing tool manufacturers over a period. Again, it really is impossible to be categorical about the correct contents and types of tool in TR tool kits.

TR5 tool kits lost the pliers/grips, the larger screwdriver and the grease gun, but gained a 'tyre valve tool' and a 'set screw' for use in removing the front hub grease caps. TR250s were provided with a more meagre kit, although it seems that a full kit could be had as an accessory. Indeed, it appears that a full kit was always available as an accessory over the whole TR4-6 production period. As standard, the TR250 was given only a sparking plug spanner, headlamp removal tool, combination tool and tyre valve tool, plus a pouch to house them and the wheel nut spanner. The tool pouch (part number 146366) rather than the full tool roll (part number 24731) also appears to have been supplied with the TR4A for the US market, suggesting that these models also had reduced tool kits like the TR250s.

European TR6s from 1969 to 1973 were usually supplied with a tool kit contained in a black plasticised roll. On one car known to be original and complete this comprised the three AF open-ended spanners and tube spanner mentioned above, plus a tommy bar, plug spanner, pliers, combination tool, small 'King Dick' adjustable spanner, front hub grease cap removal screw and feeler gauge. Parts catalogues imply that there may have been a tyre pressure gauge as well. As with TR250s, it is thought that kits on North American cars did not include the open-ended spanners (or pliers?), which would have left them including very little more than wheel-changing hardware. However, this may well have varied as factory policy changed from time to time. The general trend, of course, was moving away from supplying tools as owner maintenance of cars generally became less usual. It seems likely that non-US TR6s from 1974 onwards also had much reduced tool kits.

As for the finish of individual tools, one cannot be certain as this depended on manufacturer. Black powder-coated spanners appear to have been quite common, but there were also many left in their natural finish.

Electrics & Lamps

As with the sidescreen TRs, electrical parts were supplied almost exclusively by Lucas. In all cars, from TR4 to TR6, the 12-volt battery inhabited the space behind the engine, centrally positioned under the bonnet on a shelf forming part of the front bulkhead. On TR4s and TR4As, a 57Ah (Ampere hours) battery of type BT9A was fitted, although some early TR4s had a barely adequate 51Ah type. The battery became type C9 on TR5s and early TR6s (CZ 11/9 for cold climates), and type P130 (AZ 11 and AZ 13 for export and cold climates) on later TR6s. The battery was clamped into place by a right-angled bar, painted black and held by screwed, hook-ended rods at either side to metal plates forming part of the bulkhead. The plastic colour-coded wiring loom had push-on connectors. There was a multiplicity of minor loom changes during the TR4-6 production period, and it is not practical, unfortunately, to deal with these in detail.

Almost all TR4s and TR4As were fitted with a dynamo of type C40/1. An alternator (type 11AC) was offered as an option for TR4As, and is believed to have formed part of a 'police specification' for the late TR4 as well. It is uncertain how many cars were fitted with alternators, but it must have been relatively few. TR4s were positive earth, whereas TR4As were negative earth. A late TR4 parts catalogue does refer to a positive earth alternator fitment for the TR4 (police specification), so it appears that both positive and negative earth 11AC alternators could be found. Alternators, where specified, appear to have been fitted not on the production line, but in the Sales Conversion Department, to avoid disrupting production. The regulator box, type RB106/2, was mounted on the offside front inner wing.

TR5/250s had an alternator as standard, driven by a smaller section drive belt than had been used for the dynamo-equipped cars. The type number was 15AC, still with a separate control box of type 4TR, but the unit became 15ACR on late TR5/250s and early TR6s, this type now incorporating the control system within the alternator. On later TR6s, the alternator was uprated to 16ACR for most markets – and 17ACR and 18ACR in turn for North America (but some US cars had an AC

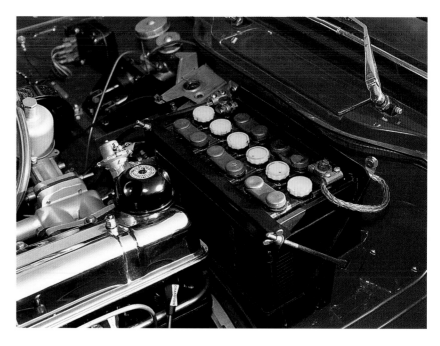

Delco unit). An optional heavy-duty alternator was also available for some other export markets. A type 4FJ fuse carrier containing 35-amp fuses was fitted to the TR4 and TR4A, replaced by type 7FJ for the six-cylinder cars. The 4FJ type had two fitted fuses and two spares, whereas the 7FJ had four fitted fuses and two spares.

Ignition coils were type HA12 on all but the later TR6s, for which type 15C6 – a six-volt coil used with a ballast resistor – was substituted. Four-

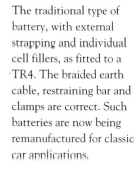

The traditional type of battery, with external strapping and individual cell fillers, as fitted to a TR4. The braided earth cable, restraining bar and clamps are correct. Such batteries are now being remanufactured for classic car applications.

Several different specifications of Lucas alternator were fitted to TR5/250/6 models, but this type is representative.

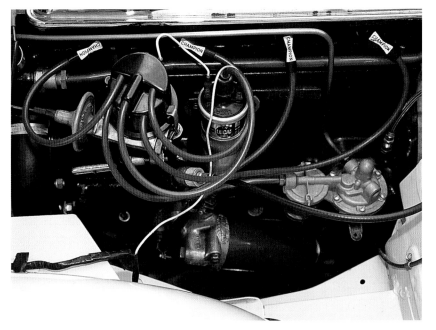

The distributor and coil seen on a TR4. The distributor cap is a later type; the original should have the Lucas name embossed on it, and is dark brown rather than black. The 'Champion' plug caps are of the correct period, but the original plug leads probably would have been black rather than red. The fuel pump and vacuum advance unit are seen clearly.

cylinder distributors were type DM2P4 for the earlier TR4s, with 25D4 being substituted on the later TR4s (from CT 17954) and all TR4As. Distributors with slightly modified internal components were supplied for both the optional 1991cc engine and the low-compression engine. Six-cylinder cars had a type 22D6 distributor, variously modified to suit local conditions. The TR250 brochure stated that the car used a 'dual vacuum advance/retard system for increased accuracy'. Champion L87Y or Lodge CNY plugs were standard for TR4/4As, while the Champion plugs in six-cylinder cars were N9Y (injection) or UN12Y (carburettors); plugs in all models used a 0.025in gap. High-tension leads were usually black, but other colours – particularly red and green – were seen on later cars. Right-angled black plastic plug connectors were usual on four-cylinder cars, although six-cylinder cars more often had straight-type plug connectors – but either type seems to be correct on TR5s and TR6s. Original equipment lead sets for TR5/6s, by Lucas

or Ripaults, usually have dark green carbon leads and black plastic end caps.

TR4/4As continued to employ the M418G inertia drive type starter motor, painted black (or sometimes red). The TR5 also used type M418G but of pre-engaged design, although an M35G/1 inertia drive type was an alternative that was also used on the TR250. Early TR6s continued to use the M418G, but later cars (from CP 53637 and CC 63845) used the pre-engaged type 2M100 starter. The type 2ST starter solenoid used on the TR4/4A was replaced on the TR5/6 by the 4ST type. Where overdrive was supplied, the overdrive relay unit was fitted for TR4/4As on the passenger side of the front bulkhead in the cockpit, and for TR5/250/6s to an under-bonnet bracket on the side wall of the inner wing near the wiper motor. Twin black-painted horns – a matched pair of high-note and low-note horns – were fitted to all of these cars. Lucas type 9H horns were more usual, but some horns were manufactured by Clear Hooters Ltd.

The TR4 was fitted as standard with single-speed, self-parking windscreen wipers, these being driven by a PS7 motor (but type DR3A was also listed) mounted on the nearside front bulkhead top, accessible from under the bonnet. The optional two-speed wiper motor was type 58SA. The TR4A had two-speed wipers as standard, but the motor was different, type DR3A, and this continued for the TR5; the TR6 motor was 14W. Many different types of wiper blades (usually 10in or 10½in) and arms were used on these cars, the original blades being of Trico manufacture. Because of the ventilation flap let into the scuttle top, one wiper arm was cranked in order to clear the flap when opened; this arrangement appears to have continued on later TR6s, even though the flap had been replaced by a fixed air inlet grille. Chromed blades and arms were used on the TR4/4A/5; although TR250s and many earlier CP and CC series TR6s had satin-finished items, some chromed ones did appear. With the introduction of the CR/CF series cars, 10in matt black

Earlier and later wiper motors are seen here. The earlier rectangular type is fitted to a TR250, and the Lucas build date of '9/67' can clearly be seen. The later TR6 type with the cylindrical motor casing was manufactured by Smiths, but its position within the car remained the same. Note the rubber buffer stop for the bonnet corner in both views.

Many early home market TR4s still had the 'tripod' style of Lucas headlamp seen on the blue car, although more common was the plain type seen on the red car. Sealed beam versions of the plain headlamp were fitted for many, but not all, markets. Correct TR4 details are the tiny sidelight lens inset into the top of the grille and the amber indicator lens in domed glass (many replacements are plastic).

wiper blades and arms were substituted to fall in with fashion. Although the TR4/4A had a manual screen wash arrangement (optional on the TR4, standard on the TR4A), the six-cylinder cars had electric washers of type 5SJ (to the end of 1972), type 9SJ (for 1973) or type 10SJ (from 1974). The spray nozzles were mounted on the bezels surrounding the wiper arm spindles.

Headlamps on TR4s, as on the TR3A, were 'block lens' type P700 for the home market, and usually F700 for export cars. A note in the TR4 brochure indicates that 'lighting arrangements were available to suit all export markets', so several different types of light unit could be found. Headlamps with 'tripod' bars were certainly fitted to earlier home market and to some export market TR4s, separate bulbs still being employed. However, later TR4s for most markets had sealed beam units. Chromed front rims were fitted to the headlamps, in addition to the chromed-edge inner rims, with black neoprene gaskets and dust excluders. Bulbs were initially 36/60-watt.

TR4As all used sealed beam units, the Lucas type number F700 appearing to cover all applications despite the fact that these units clearly differ from earlier F700 types. This F700 designation, in fact, appears to cover all headlamps fitted through to the end of the TR6. Although different lens patterns were used to cater for various export markets, Lucas did not see fit to number the different units individually, which makes things difficult for those aspiring to exact originality. Due to supply problems for a brief period in August 1972, some TR6s were fitted with GEC headlamp units, either in pairs or mixed with Lucas units. The dipswitch remained the floor-mounted and foot-operated type 103SA until late 1972, when

this archaic practice finally gave way on the CR/CF series TR6s to a hand-operated switch mounted on the left of the steering column.

TR4 sidelights were very small Lucas type 658 items with frosted plastic lenses, fitted outboard of the headlamps and let into the top corners of the grille. Separate type 594 amber flasher lights, with the usual domed glass lens and chromed bezel, were fitted to TR4/4A/5/250 models and again let into the grille, this time at each bottom

At some point during TR4 production, the Lucas tail lamp changed from type 669 (above left), with a circular pattern on the amber and lower red lenses, to type 799 (above right), with a vertical pattern on these lenses.

The TR4A/5/250 received a new sidelight unit (above), combined with a repeater amber flasher visible from the side. All TR5s and TR250s had twin reversing lamps (right) as standard, this being the type employed. Each lamp was mounted on a plinth below the rear light unit.

Into both rear overriders on the TR4/4A/5/250 were built these small number plate illumination lamps. The tiny lenses were glass, and the wiring passed up inside the overrider itself.

TR250s had red marker lights on the rear wings, as did the TR5 even though legislation did not normally require them. The red lens correctly has a screw only at one end, a clip securing the other.

corner. Clear rather than amber lenses were fitted for some export markets. The flasher unit was type FL5 on the TR4/4A, 8FL on the TR5/250. The TR4A/5/250 had the type 658 front sidelight combined with a flasher repeater unit (type 771) in a chromed moulding at the front of each wing, this moulding forming the front section of the side flash added to these cars. A hazard warning light system appeared for the first time on most left-hand drive TR5s and all TR250s, but this was not found on home market TR5s or on some left-hand drive TR5s.

For the TR6 entirely new combined flasher and front side/marker light units (type 827) were fitted in the front valance above the bumper. The unit fitted to North American cars had an all-amber lens, with one twin-filament bulb serving both sidelight and indicator functions, whereas cars for other markets had an amber/clear lens with two separate single-filament bulbs. Flashing indicator repeater lights (type 844) were fitted to the front wings forward of the wheel arches, although type 826, incorporating reflector units, were fitted to US specification cars. Late US specification cars had entirely different front flashers/sidelights, these having to be hung below the front bumper both to allow room for the black 'safety' overriders and because the raised front bumper would have partially obscured the lights in the original position. US TR6s had clear sidelights and flashers for the 1975 model year, whereas both lenses were amber on 1976 cars.

Rear lamps appear identical on the TR4/4A/5/250 models, being a combined reflector, brake light, tail light and direction indicator unit. A deep chromed bezel surrounded the whole, with a separate horizontal chromed bar dividing the orange flasher lens (on home market cars) at the top from the central reflector. In fact, the tail light and indicator lenses on late TR4s, TR4As, TR5/250s featured a vertical embossed pattern (type 799), whereas those on earlier TR4s had a circular 'swirl' pattern (type 669). No precise change point has been uncovered for this alteration. North American cars had red rather than amber rear flasher lenses to comply with local legislation. Reversing lights (type 661) were listed as optional on TR4s and TR4As, but the TR5/250 had standard reversing lights (type 594) with domed frosted glass lenses and chromed bezels, mounted below the rear light units. Number plate illumination on TR4/4A/5/250s was provided by two chromed, domed type 550 units, one let into each rear overrider, where they also usefully illuminated the luggage area with the boot opened. German market TR4/4A/5s had the TR3A type of number plate light and special plain overriders. The TR5/250 had rear red marker lights (type 734) sited low down on the rear wings.

Two differing patterns of sidelight/indicator unit were fitted to TR6s. The 'above-bumper' type (far left) was used for all markets to the end of the 1974 model year, when regulations requiring increased bumper height necessitated new units below the bumper on US cars. Headlamps and side indicator repeater lamps remained similar throughout production.

TR6 rear lamp units did not change during production, but legislation required the wrapped-round part of the indicator to be red on US cars.

Entirely new type 832 rear light assemblies were fitted to the TR6. These were of 'strip' pattern, the outer lamp being the flasher which wrapped round the rear corners of the car, thus avoiding the need for repeater flashers at the rear. The TR5/250 rear marker lights were also deleted. The amber lens was changed to red for North American cars. At the inner end of each of these light units were reversing lights, while in the middle were the stop/tail lamp unit and a square reflex reflector. A chromed bezel surrounded the whole light unit. Number plate illumination on the TR6 was originally by a chromed 'strip' light (type 766) mounted on top of the rear bumper, but the CR/CF series cars had a pair of lights (type 908) fitted to the recess above the rear registration/licence plate area.

The TR6 finally saw an interior light added to the specification, by having a tunnel-mounted light and switch combined, together with a glovebox light. This continued until the introduction of the CR/CF series saw twin interior lights, one shining into each footwell, operated by a switch mounted on the gear lever console and courtesy switches on each A post. TR6s also possessed a small boot light positioned in the front 'wall' of the boot interior under a translucent plastic cover, operated by raising the boot lid.

Earlier CP/CC series TR6s were fitted with this style of chromed number plate lamp housing on the rear bumper. Later cars had the plate lit from above, by two flush-fitting lamps at the top of the number plate recess.

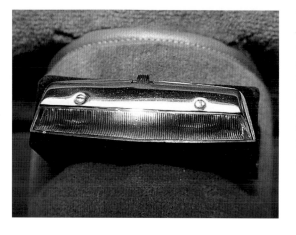

The single interior courtesy lamp of the earlier TR6s was mounted on the rear of the transmission tunnel – not an ideal position for map-reading! This was replaced by a light in each footwell for the CR/CF series models.

Engine

The TR4/4A used Triumph's classic four-cylinder engine in 86mm bore form, giving 2138cc (130.5cu in). The old 1991cc variant from sidescreen TRs, with 83mm bore, remained available to special order. Derived from the Standard Vanguard, this engine had been refined over many years to reach something of a plateau of development in the TR3A, and thus little needed to be done for the TR4/4A application other than fitting a new front plate to allow for the new model's engine mountings, which were further apart.

The four-cylinder TR engine was of wet-liner construction, the pistons running in pressed-in nickel chrome steel liners rather than directly in the block. The liners were surrounded as far as practicable by a water jacket that was sealed at the top by the head gasket and at the base by 'figure of eight' gaskets. The advantages of such con-struction are better cooling, the ease with which worn liners can be replaced and the simplicity with which the cubic capacity can be changed.

The flat-topped pistons were made of alu-minium alloy, and had two compression rings and one oil scraper ring. The standard TR4/4A capac-ity of 2138cc gave a compression ratio of 9:1, although for export markets where only low-grade fuel was available 7.5:1 or even 7:1 could be spec-ified to special order. This reduction was achieved by means of a compression plate inserted between the head and the block. Piston and liner sets of 87mm, 89mm and even 92mm bore are available today, enabling capacity to be taken up to 2½ litres, but the biggest size can lead to overheating and other related problems, and should be treated with caution. The most commonly used replace-ment size today seems to be 87mm.

The immaculate engine bay of a concours TR4, showing the earlier type of inlet manifold and SU H6 carburettors, correctly fitted with brass caps to the dashpots. A chromed rocker cover is correct on any TR4/4A.

The block was cast iron with a sheet steel sump beneath, although a cast aluminium one was available as an option. The crankshaft was carried in three main bearings, which, like the big-end bearings, featured precision-machined, steel-backed, white metal bearing shells. The crankshaft itself was a molybdenum manganese steel forging, cross-drilled to ensure adequate lubrication under hard usage. The crankshaft rear was sealed with a scroll-type seal (which is prone to leaking) and at the front within the timing cover was a conventional oil seal.

A duplex chain drove the camshaft, which in turn drove the distributor and oil pump by skew gears, and also activated the mechanical fuel pump. The camshaft had four bearings, and drove the eight vertical overhead valves by means of tappets, pushrods and rockers, the inlet valves having double springs and the exhaust valves triple springs. Exhaust valves were of 1.30in diameter, inlet valves 1.56in. The cylinder head had eight ports – four inlet and four exhaust – on the left hand side (looking from the front of the engine) along with the dynamo and starter; the fuel pump, oil filter, distributor and spark plugs were on the right-hand side. The head was of what is known in TR circles as 'high-port' design, as compared with the TR2/3 'low-port' type. Valve timing on the TR4 was conservative for a sports car at 15°/55°/55°/15°, and valve lift was 0.375in.

The crankcase on the early TR4 engine was vented by a breather formed from a right-angled pipe, internally baffled, and mounted low down on the rear of the block, on the distributor side. At the forward end of the block on the same side was found the 'bent-wire' dipstick, which passed into the crankcase via a hole in a cast boss. Dipstick position is a good guide to a correct TR engine (other than engine number), for blocks cast for saloons, tractors and other applications have their dipstick holes further back, although the 'TR position' boss is still there, undrilled. It is not unknown for four-cylinder TRs to have had these 'lesser' engines substituted for correct TR ones over the years, and purchasers of TR4/4As should always check for this. The other engines have smaller head studs, different cylinder heads and generally inferior bearing, lubrication and other specifications. The 'CT' engine number prefix should always be checked, although engine number stampings can frequently be very difficult to decipher. The number is stamped on a milled flat surface to the right of the coil mounting point, near the top of the block.

Power output for the TR4 engine was quoted as 100bhp net (105bhp gross), with maximum torque of 127lb ft at 3350rpm. The safe maximum engine speed was considered to be 5000rpm, although occasional bursts up to 5500rpm appear to do no harm. The TR engine benefits greatly

The other side of the four-cylinder engine, showing the fuel pump and distributor. Original plug leads would probably have been black rather than red, and the correct colour of the early type of oil filler cap/breather is much debated – black or silver would appear to be correct. This car incorrectly carries the later TR4/4A inlet manifold which normally went with Stromberg carburettors, except on late TR4As.

Stromberg 175CD carburettors are seen on this late TR4, together with the later type of TR4 air cleaners and recirculating breather system. Also seen is the later rocker cover with the 'eared' type of oil filler cap.

The 'Purolator' oil filter canister is seen here. Several different colours are known, and the green shown here is probably close to an original shade.

from careful balancing and this is a worthwhile modification to incorporate into a rebuild. A full-flow oil filter system with a filter by either Automotive Products or Tecalemit was utilised, the Tecalemit type being more usual on TR4As. The two types are interchangeable, but only as complete units, as the individual components all differ. Standard oil pressure was quoted as 'between 40 and 60lb/sq in when the car is travelling at normal speeds and the oil is hot'. However, TR4/4A engines will run for many thousands of miles showing lower pressures than these, and cases of incorrectly reading gauges are common. Oil capacity (from dry), including the

filter, is 11 pints, although fitting the optional (deeper) cast aluminium sump increases this to approximately 12½ pints.

To the nose of the crankshaft was bolted the dynamo/water pump driving belt pulley, plus a cast extension piece that carried the balanced and vibration-absorbing cooling fan. A large bolt passed through the extension piece into the crankshaft, and on TR4s this carried a starting handle dog, deleted on the TR4A. The dog was in place on TR4 engines whether or not the optional starting handle had been requested. The engine mounts for TR4s differed from the earlier TR 'rectangular' type in that they were a cylindrical rubber/metal 'sandwich', with a retention bracket, which was later deleted. At an unknown point during the TR4A's run, the cylindrical type was deleted in favour of a return to the rectangular type, only this time of a 'fail-safe' design. The two types of mountings are interchangeable, but only in pairs.

Modifications to the reliable and well-tried four-cylinder engine during the TR4/4A period were few. At CT 14233E, a rocker cover with a closed circuit breather was incorporated. The TR4 rocker cover had its filler/breather cap at the bulkhead end of the engine rather than at the forward end, as found on the TR3A, but rocker covers of the earlier pattern were probably fitted to a few early TR4s. The 'open-circuit' breather

Two views, one from each side, of a superbly detailed fuel injection TR5 engine bay. The large plastic brake fluid reservoir is visible, coupled to the direct-acting servo unit. A chromed rocker cover is correct on this car, and the position of the commission plate, riveted to a wheel arch, can be seen.

The TR250 engine bay, again seen from both sides, looks less full than the TR5 one. The emission control Stromberg carburettors are on view, together with their elongated oval air cleaner unit which contained two separate, renewable elements. The yellow and black brake servo hose passes from the manifold over the engine, these colours being correct for the hoses on TR250s.

was painted black with a 'recommended oils' transfer in white, whereas the later closed-circuit type oil filler cap looked more like a radiator cap, painted silver, and with a metered valve which allowed air to be sucked in. The only major change to the four-cylinder motor occurred just over halfway through the TR4's run at CT 21471E, at the same time as Stromberg carburettors replaced the SU type (see 'Carburettors & Fuel Injection', page 75). At this point, a revised cylinder head (part number 511695) was introduced, having reshaped combustion chambers with better gas-flow characteristics. In conjunction with this came a new design of inlet manifold, with Y-shaped inlets from carburettors to ports, again leading to improved gas flow. Power output must have improved, but 100bhp net (105bhp gross) remained quoted.

The final factory development of the four-cylinder engine arrived with the TR4A in March 1965. In addition to the new cylinder head and inlet manifold described above, this also had a cast four-into-two exhaust manifold (see 'Exhaust System', page 84) and a camshaft with slightly revised timing (17°/57°/57°/17°) to match the new manifolds. Distributor changes were also introduced as a consequence of these modifications. Power output was now quoted at 104bhp net. Crankcase breathing became a fully closed-circuit system, and a Smiths 'Anti-Smog' valve was incorporated into the breathing arrangements. This valve maintained crankcase suction at the correct level, and also doubled as a flame trap. Late TR4s with the earlier closed-circuit breathing and all TR4As also dispensed with wire mesh air filters, having instead twin paper element filters painted silver, with an oval drum shape. Apart from the reversion to SU carburettors (still retaining the new manifolds), there were no further significant specification changes to the four-cylinder engine.

Some controversy surrounds the colour in which engines were painted. The great majority were finished in black, and a black-painted TR4/4A engine could not, I think, be criticised. However, examples purporting to be original are known in dark blue, red and a kind of sea green. Factory rebuild exchange engines often appeared in such colours, and one cannot be categorical in ruling out a particular colour. Cylinder heads matched engine blocks, and brackets, fittings and ancillaries, where painted, were usually black or in some cases, such as thermostat housings and carburettors, left as cast or mildly polished. Rocker covers were always polished chrome.

By the mid-'60s, it was obvious to Triumph that a major increase in power output would be needed to ensure that the TR's healthy sales record continued. Following two false starts – the first with the expensive twin-cam 'Sabrina' engine and the second with a 'stretched' 2½-litre version of the existing engine with 'dry' cylinder liners – the decision was taken to develop a more reliably powerful version of the company's six-cylinder 2-litre engine which had already been used for rallying in tuned form in the works Triumph 2000 saloons. This six-cylinder engine had first been seen in the Standard Vanguard 'Vignale' Six of 1959/60 and was later fitted to the production Triumph 2000. Its origins lay in the Standard '8' four-cylinder economy saloon of 1953: by progressively stretching the bore size, adding two cylinders and finally increasing the stroke, what had started as a 26bhp 803cc engine became a 150bhp 2498cc unit!

Unlike the wet-liner TR2-4A engine, the TR5/250/6 engine was dry-linered and of very conventional construction. Both block and head were of cast iron with a high chrome content, and a new design of 12-port head was developed specially for the TR application. The crankshaft ran in four main bearings and the camshaft was driven by duplex chain from the crankshaft nose. The Lucas 22D6 distributor, fuel metering unit and oil pump were propelled by a skew gear driven shaft from the camshaft, while the water pump and newly-introduced alternator were belt driven from the crankshaft, which itself carried a plastic fan on an extension piece. Flat-top aluminium alloy pistons were fitted, each with two chromed compression rings and two scraper rings, the latter separated by a spacer. Conventional rocker gear and 12 overhead valves were driven by tappets and upright pushrods, double valve springs being fitted. Exhaust valves were 'Stellite' faced. The AC full-flow oil filter system was mounted directly onto the right-hand side of the block, below the distributor. A new high-capacity oil pump was developed for this engine, of eccentric lobe design, which did not lose pressure when worn, unlike the gear-driven types.

The fuel injection car's compression ratio was 9.5:1, but 8.6:1 was used for the carburettor version. Bore and stroke were 74.7mm and 95.0mm respectively, tappet clearance was 0.010in both for inlet and exhaust valves, and fuel injection allowed valve timing that was verging on the wild at 35°/65°/65°/35°. The resultant power output was quoted as 150bhp net and maximum torque of 164lb ft occurred at 3000rpm. The carburettor TR250 suffered considerably, with maximum power of 104bhp net (the same as the TR4A) and peak torque of 143lb ft at 3500rpm. A milder camshaft was fitted, timed at 10°/50°/50°/10°. The TR250 brochure described this camshaft as being of 'hyposine' design!

This engine was modified only in minor detail during the 15-month production run of the

Two views of a superb late CP series TR6 fuel injection engine, correct in virtually every detail. By 1970, the chromed rocker cover had given way to this plainer painted one. Note the neat grouping of the fuel injection leads with 'fir tree' connectors. The fuel metering unit is clearly visible.

TR5/250 and was virtually unchanged for early TR6s. However, for some reason the crankshaft cross-drillings on the bearing journals of the injected TR6 engines were deleted from CP 52320 onwards; this probably also applied to the carburettor engines as well, but the factory service bulletin does not make this clear. As is well-known, difficulties in keeping the injected engines in tune, a desire to improve emission characteristics and general customer complaints all forced Triumph to detune the injected engine at the end of 1972, at the introduction of the CR series cars. The camshaft was replaced by a much milder 18°/58°/58°/18° item, although the compression ratio stayed at 9.5:1. The result was a better-tempered but slower car, 124bhp at the then new DIN measurement being quoted.

Carburettor TR6s initially used the TR250 engine, but in late 1970 the 18°/58°/58°/18° camshaft was introduced, together with a reduction in compression ratio to 7.75:1. Compression ratio dropped further to 7.5:1 in late 1974. These 'federalised' North American cars also suffered from an exhaust gas recirculation system, and finally an air injection pump was added to further

clean up the exhaust. Numerous other engine and carburation changes were made to comply with US legislation, but the details are too complex to be dealt with in the space available.

On injected engines, the block fitting for a camshaft-operated fuel pump was blanked off, but this was used on carburettor cars for an AC mechanical pump. These latter cars had a conventional air cleaner system consisting of a single elongated oval canister containing two disposable elements, the canister, painted silver, being bolted direct to the carburettors. The injected cars had a drum-type filter mounted to one side of the radiator, this feeding into a cylindrical air collection gallery which in turn fed the inlet manifold via six wire-clipped hoses.

Engine blocks were usually painted black with silver-painted rocker covers, although these have often been subsequently chromed; TR5s, TR250s and 1969 model year TR6s had chromed covers as standard. Most ancillaries were left in the colours as supplied by their manufacturers; the air collection gallery cylinder was painted matt black, whereas the air cleaner drum on injected cars was either matt silver or matt black.

A very late US-specification carburettor TR6 sporting the full panoply of emission control equipment, including the belt-driven air pump mounted above the alternator.

Carburettors & Fuel Injection

The TR4 started its production run with the traditional twin SU set-up, retaining the TR3A's H6 type 1¾in carburettors complete with brass dashpot caps and offset wire mesh air cleaners, which were usually painted black but sometimes silver. However, push-on rubber connectors were now used in the petrol pipe runs and no fuel shut-off tap was fitted. It is a good idea to use clips on the push-on petrol pipes, a slight loss of originality being much more preferable to a fire! The black-painted fuel tank, of 11¾ gallons capacity, was sited in a lateral position under the rear bulkhead, a rubber pipe projecting upwards from the top of the tank towards the rear deck panel to connect with the traditional TR snap-action filler cap. The tank was vented at the top by a separate vent pipe attached via a banjo connection. The standard carburettor needles were SU type SM, no change having been necessary with the increase in engine capacity to 2138cc. Fuel continued to be pumped by a camshaft-driven AC pump, and the chokes were operated manually by Bowden cable from the dashboard. From CT 19970 the petrol tank itself and the filler cap and neck assembly changed, with the deletion of the separate tank vent pipe and the incorporation of the vent into the cap itself, but the two types were interchangeable. With the introduction of the first closed-circuit breathing system at engine number CT 14233E, drum type paper element air cleaners were fitted, connected by a Y-shaped tube to an outlet pipe on the redesigned rocker cover.

The use of 1¾in SUs continued until engine number CT 16800E, at which point a trial run of 100 cars was produced with Stromberg type 175CD 1¾in constant vacuum carburettors. It seems that Triumph wanted to fit this carburettor, based on the SU principle, purely because it was manufactured by an independent concern, and not, as with the SU, by its arch-rival, the British Motor Corporation! It was also rumoured that SU carburettors cost Triumph twice as much as they cost MG! Although a redesigned and improved inlet manifold was introduced with these carburettors, as detailed in the 'Engine' section (see page 72), the attachment points remained identical, so either type of carburettor fits either manifold. The manifold incorporated a take-off in connection with the closed-circuit breathing system. Twin oval-shaped paper element air filters were now fitted, the elements being of the disposable type, made by AC. A stick-on paper decal detailing patent arrangements adorned the filters, the colour of which varied, although blue was quite common. For some reason, possibly contractual, a complete changeover to Strombergs did not take place for a further few months, but from engine number CT 21471E all TR4s had the new carburettors and manifolds as standard, together with the revised cylinder head described in the 'Engine' section.

Two views of the SU H6 carburettors fitted to earlier TR4s, showing the brass dashpot damper tops and the original style of gauze air filters. Push-fit fuel lines with no securing clips are correct, although many owners prefer the security of non-original clipped fixings. This is the early inlet manifold, used to mid-1963.

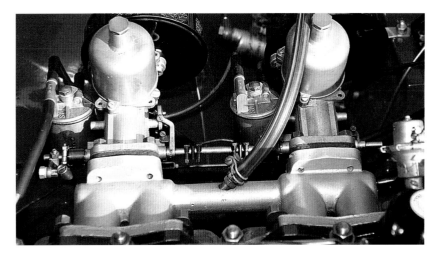

A pair of later SU HS6 carburettors with black plastic dashpot damper tops, mounted on the later type of inlet manifold, with less obstructed inlet passages. A highly polished finish such as this would not be original, and the fuel lines, although in period, are also incorrect. Note the small brass pipe connecting carburettors to vacuum advance mechanism.

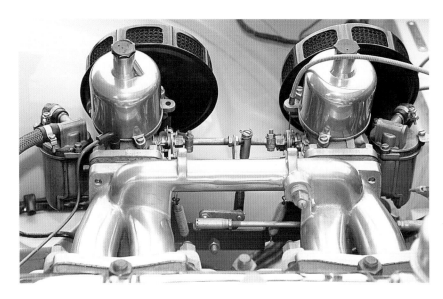

A late TR4 engine (below) showing Stromberg carburettors and drum air cleaners (with renewable elements), which replaced the gauze versions. The blue colour of the air cleaners is probably correct, although other colours were also used.

Strombergs were used well into the TR4A's production run, but at commission number CT 62191 SUs became standard again, still on the improved manifold. This change may well have been prompted because the formation of the British Leyland Motor Corporation meant that SUs were no longer supplied by a rival, but were now manufactured within the group of which Triumph had become a part. The SUs were now the updated HS6 type, with black plastic dashpot caps and improved petrol feed arrangements between the float chambers and the carburettor bodies. The standard needle changed to type TW. The oval-shaped paper element air filters continued from the Strombergs on to the SUs, and the parts catalogue lists an additional 'air cleaner and silencer assembly', part number 212273, stated to be for special order only. In this system, the same paper element filters were enclosed in an elongated oval metal box with parallel sides, but how many cars actually sported this arrangement, and why it was considered necessary, remains unclear. The fuel system on the TR4A otherwise remained similar to the TR4 installation, except for pipework, clip and throttle linkage changes which had become necessary because of the carburettor and manifold substitutions. A rigid fuel pipe was used to connect the two carburettors in the TR4A SU application.

Upon its introduction in 1967, the TR5 became the first British series production car to be fitted with fuel injection. In fact, it is not widely known that, prior to this, a fuel injection system for the four-cylinder TR4A engine was developed by Tecalemit-Jackson working with Triumph's engineers. Although prototype cars existed and ran, the system never reached production.

The introduction of fuel injection – 'petrol injection' as the factory preferred to call it – for the TR5 allowed the use of a camshaft with a more advanced and wilder profile than would otherwise

An unrestored TR4A engine, showing what is assumed to be the 'special order' air cleaner/silencer assembly, within which the separate renewable elements were contained. The 'one-way' valve that formed part of the breather system is visible to the right of the heater control tap. A non-original plastic fan, possibly from a TR250, is fitted.

The heart of the fuel injection system, the metering unit, can be seen on a TR6 (above) to the right of and below the distributor. From this, the injection pipes pass over the engine to the inlet side. Fuel injection inlet manifolds, air collection chamber, air inlet hoses and feed pipe from the air cleaner drum are all visible in the TR5 view (right). Only the outer air inlet hoses are clipped in position, the inner four relying on a push fit. Also seen is the cable-operated throttle mechanism; the correct colour of the cable is debated but black seems acceptable.

have been possible, so that power output grew sufficiently for the TR to remain competitive in performance terms. Triumph wished to use a British injection system and only Lucas was offering anything ready for production – but development continued in the hands of the first customers!

The heart of the system was the shuttle-type fuel metering unit, driven by gearing from the distributor drive shaft and bolted to the left-hand side of the engine between the distributor and the bulkhead. This unit received petrol at high pressure from the tank via a fuel filter assembly and a specially developed Lucas fuel pump. This was electrically powered for the first time on a TR, and on the earliest production cars – only the first 24, it is believed – the pump was sited in the engine compartment. However, excessive heat in this position soon caused problems with fuel vaporisation, so the pump was quickly repositioned in the boot, and the early cars were rapidly modified in this way under warranty. Nevertheless, vaporisation problems have persisted ever since in hot weather, despite the addition of cooling coils to the pump and other modifications.

From the mechanical metering unit, fuel was fed via six plastic pipes to the individual injectors, which were retained by a keeper plate bolted to the manifold. The injectors had screwed-on insulators. There were three inlet manifolds, each having two ports to give an individual entry passage for each cylinder. Air was introduced to each cylinder via six pipes connected to the manifolds from an air collection reservoir cylinder fed from the air cleaner drum. Fuel was pumped constantly at a consistent pressure from the tank, there being a return pipe system so that fuel not required by the engine at any given moment was returned to the tank for re-circulation. A cold start knob was fitted, which opened the throttles and caused the metering unit to deliver a richer mixture. Throttle control was achieved by a cable, bell crank and countershaft arrangement. Apart from the initial change of pump position, and despite the tuning and other problems that arose, the injection system was little modified during TR5 production. However, shortly after production ceased, a dealer-fitted modification – the incorporation of an air bleed valve into the system – was made available, from 1 November 1968. TR5s could be retrospectively fitted with this modification free of charge, and it seems that most were. All TR6s had inlet manifold air bleeds incorporated from the start.

Due, allegedly, to increasingly severe exhaust emission regulations then becoming enforced in the USA, cars for North America were not sold with the fuel injection system, which, somewhat surprisingly, could not be made to meet the requirements. As a result the TR250 was pro-

duced, these cars having the new six-cylinder engine with twin emission-controlled Stromberg 175 CD carburettors which could, by careful tuning, be made to meet the new regulations. The bad news was that power output at 104bhp net was no higher than the TR4A's, although maximum torque improved to 143lb ft. The good news was that the cost of this carburettor system was very much lower, and this may well have been the true reason why the injection car was not sold in North America. Frankly, it has always seemed implausible that a fuel injection system could not be made to meet exhaust emission controls.

A new 'two-into-six' one-piece inlet manifold was developed, water-heated by a pipe from the water pump. An AC mechanical fuel pump was used, with just a single fuel line from the tank and a small plastic in-line fuel filter. A conventional choke mechanism was fitted. The fuel tank itself was very similar to the TR4A type, but all three tanks for the TR4A/5/250 differed in detail. Quoted capacities differ depending upon which source one believes – 11¼, 11½ and 11¾ gallons are all mentioned. As a sales ploy, all TR250s had

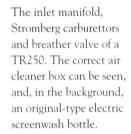

The inlet manifold, Stromberg carburettors and breather valve of a TR250. The correct air cleaner box can be seen, and, in the background, an original-type electric screenwash bottle.

This transfer, seen on a TR250, should be fitted to the air cleaner box.

The carburettor side of a late North American specification TR6 fitted with full emission control equipment. The air pump can be seen on the far side of the engine, above the radiator top hose. On some late TR6s reimported into the UK in recent years, this emission control equipment has a tendency to work loose and fall off! Late Stromberg carburettors have gold rather than black damper tops.

A plate detailing engine tuning information and certifying compliance with 1974 regulations is seen on a North American TR6.

large 'Monza' type fuel filler caps held closed magnetically. These may also have been fitted to a few export TR5s, it seems, and were also found on North American specification TR6s.

The TR6 used the same basic injection system as the TR5, but with some modifications in addition to the air bleed detailed above. The pressure relief valve, for instance, was moved from its former chassis-mounted position to a less vulnerable location within the boot. During 1972, the insulators on the injectors changed from being the screwed-on type to being a push fit, although the injectors themselves remained the same as the TR5 type. From the introduction of the detuned CR series cars at the end of 1972, the inlet manifolds, linkages, metering unit, pipes and clips all changed to suit the new engine specification. The TR6 fuel tank differed slightly from that of the TR5, and it was again modified from CP 50001 to stop fuel surge, which was causing problems with the engine cutting out. The air intake manifold was also modified at CP 50001, although the air cleaner assembly and element remained the same throughout. At least four fuel metering pumps,

differing in detail, were used on the TR6, and a special 'high altitude' metering unit was available on cars for certain markets. The fuel pump itself remained unchanged, and the fuel filter continued to use the same element, but the filter unit itself differed slightly from the TR5 one. The later TR6 injection system incorporated an inertia switch to cut off the fuel supply in severe impact. Three different TR6 fuel filler caps are listed, one of which is the TR5 type, which in turn differed from the TR4/4A type – but the records do not reveal which type was fitted when.

The TR6 carburettor cars again used the constant-vacuum, emission-controlled Strombergs with a single fuel line and engine-driven AC pump. Four inlet manifolds differing in detail were fitted at different times as follows: up to engine number CC 50000HE, from CC 50001HE to CC 75000HE, from CC 75001HE to CF 1HE, and from CF 1HE onwards. From CC 50001HE, a petrol vapour absorption device was fitted in addition to the emission-control system. The carburettor assemblies changed in detail several times, change points being given as up to CC 50000HE, from CC 50001HE to CC 65346HE, from CC 65347HE to CF 1HE, and from CF 1HE onwards. In the last few years of production of the carburettor TR6, a plethora of emission-control equipment was fitted, full details of which are both too complex and too lengthy to review here. When such cars are reimported into the UK, this equipment is usually the first to 'fall off' and find its way into a dark corner of the owner's garage...

The great majority of TR6s built were carburettor cars, and these in fact remained in production for the US market for more than a year after the final injected cars were built in February 1975. The last carburettor cars were built in July 1976, exactly 23 years after the first production TR2s.

As for finishes, carburettors and inlet manifolds were left as natural metal, and possibly lightly polished, and several fuel injection components were painted black, the air collection reservoir cylinder usually having a 'crackle' finish. Metering units can be a mixture of black and silver. Air cleaner drums should also be black on injection cars, although on carburettor cars air cleaner/silencer components can be black or silver.

Several ways of neatly grouping the individual pipes to each fuel injector were tried. Very early TR5s had a rubber strap arrangement, but before long 'fir tree' connectors, so named because of their shape when opened out, came into use. From around 1971 to late 1974, three 'fir tree' connectors were used, but the last injection cars built from late 1974 to early 1975 had a plastic clip arrangement, the clips being attached to two tags fixed to the rocker cover. One clip held four injector leads, the other held two.

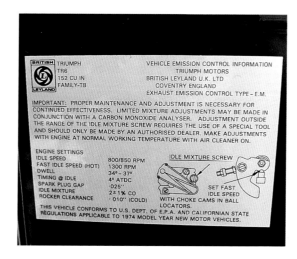

Cooling System & Heater

The TR4 was introduced with a radiator block virtually identical to that used in the sidescreen cars, this being part number 401869. The long, backwards-facing header tank with filler orifice was retained, even though there was no longer any need for this as the TR4's bodywork did not shroud the radiator, unlike that of the TR3A. Also retained was the hole in the centre of the radiator for the starting handle to pass through. The handle was still available on the TR4, but now as an optional extra. The presence of this hole cut off proper water flow through several of the radiator's tubes, impeding efficiency, so radiators without the central hole soon appeared, although fitting of either type appears to have continued at random for some time. I have been told of a TR4 which was supplied with the optional starting handle as requested by the customer but which came with a radiator lacking the central hole! There were also two types of central hole, one almost square, the other much more elongated, about twice as high as it was wide.

The radiator was attached by brackets on its lower sides to the chassis, and by two screwed and adjustable stays from its top corners passing to the bolted tubular chassis cross-member between the suspension towers. Packing pieces under the side brackets allowed for top hose outlet position adjustment. From car CT 9553, the largely redundant header tank was deleted, the redesigned radiator having its filler cap conventionally located on the radiator top. The post-CT 9553 radiator with no header tank occurs both with and without the starting handle hole, the hole always being the elongated type. The radiator with the hole is part number 402001, that without is part number 134456. A ducting shroud made of a composition material, which was prone to rapid deterioration, was fitted in front of the radiator and behind the grille. This ensured that cooling air was forced along the correct path through the radiator.

A short section of top hose, convoluted to allow for engine movement, connected the radiator to the cast aluminium thermostat housing bolted to the top front of the cylinder head. A by-pass route was incorporated. The bottom hose was in three parts, comprising two rubber hoses and a

slightly cranked steel pipe connecting them, and ran from the water pump to the radiator. Hose clips should for originality be the wire type rather than the worm-drive type. Conventional water pump circulation was used, the water pump being bolted to the front of the cylinder block and driven by a wide V belt from the crankshaft, the belt also driving the dynamo. The thermostat was usually an 82°C one for home markets, but 88°C versions were supplied for cold climates and some hot climates would have had thermostats with a lower opening temperature. The cooling system was pressurised at 4psi, although later TR4s and all TR4As had this raised to 7psi. The cooling system capacity of the TR4 (with heater) was 14 pints. For drainage purposes a brass block tap and a similar brass radiator drain tap were fitted, but the latter was later deleted in favour of a cheaper (and nastier) plug. If a heater was not specified, screwed blanking plugs were fitted to the cylinder head outlet and the water pump.

The two different types of TR4 radiator, that on the red car being the early version with the backwards-extending header tank. Wire hose clips (rather than worm-drive) are correct on cars of this age. The thermostat housing can be seen, with the electrical sender for the temperature gauge installed. Also note the fibre composition air deflector in place on both cars.

The heater control tap on a TR4.

The fan, which was balanced, was driven direct from the nose of the crankshaft via an extension piece to which it was bolted. It acted as a vibration damper, being mounted by four small rubber and steel bushes surrounding the attachment bolts. It had four blades and was usually of 12½in diameter, although small variations in fans occurred. Some had blades with squared-off ends, whereas others had the more rounded type commonly found on the sidescreen cars.

Owners who substitute electric fans should be aware that broken crankshafts can result from the loss of the damping effect of the mechanical fan, unless the engine itself has been carefully balanced. The normal running temperature of the engine should be 185°F (85°C), and a cooling system in good condition should have no trouble in keeping the temperature down to this level. The temperature gauge sender was electrical, and fitted into the side of the thermostat housing. However, it appears that some of the very earliest TR4s had the old TR3A type of capillary temperature gauge, with the consequent use of the earlier type of thermostat housing.

There are three common but easily overlooked causes of overheating on the four-cylinder TR4/4A engine. The first is the absence of the ducting shroud ahead of the radiator. The second is the use of the wrong thermostat, the correct type, which is now very hard to find, having a 'bypass blanking ring' to ensure that the bypass hose route is cut off once the thermostat opens; most modern replacements lack this, allowing water to continue to circulate via the bypass route and avoid passing through the radiator. The third is the result of some after-market replacement water pumps containing a shallower impeller which simply does not pump the water so well, so one should be sure that any replacement pump has an impeller to original specification.

The TR4 incorporated for the first time in a TR a Smiths fresh air heater, rated at 2.5kw, and this same unit was retained for the TR4A. The heater was fed by a vent (which could be closed) on top of the scuttle and sat behind the dashboard below this point. A fan blower motor was fitted. Unlike the earlier cars, all controls, including the hot water valve, could be operated from the driver's seat. The hot water control was linked to the valve itself by Bowden cable, the valve being sited at the rear of the cylinder head. The heater unit and ducting should be painted black. Demisting vents were incorporated, air flow to these, or to the cockpit area, being controlled by a dashboard knob. The demister hoses were of convoluted black plastic with wire reinforcement. The heater water passed back into the cooling system via a flexible hose and rigid pipe that connected back into the water pump.

The TR4A had a different radiator block which was wider than both of the TR4 types. Water capacity was reduced to 11 pints with the heater, and the starting handle hole in the radiator finally disappeared, for this option had been deleted. Different radiator support stays were used, these bolting to the side of the radiator and taking the form of flat plates rather than screwed rods. A 'no-loss' arrangement for the TR4A consisted of a plastic pipe from the filler neck leading into a bottle mounted low down at the side of the radiator. Some confusion exists over the types of fan fitted to the TR4A. Earlier cars were usually fitted with a six-blade metal fan, although some early cars were definitely sold new with the TR4 four-blade type. At some unknown point during the TR4A's run the six-blade fan was discontinued, the four-blade one becoming the norm. One presumes that the six-blade fan absorbed more power, and that the four-blade one was substituted because it was found that it still worked adequately well with the smaller capacity radiator. The parts catalogue in addition lists an eight-blade plastic fan for the TR4A, but fails to indicate any start point for its use. The former TR4/4A Registrar of the TR Register, after perusing many records and cars, doubts that any production TR4As ever had plastic fans, and confirms that the final production TR4A left the factory with a four-blade metal fan.

The radiator and associated brackets should be painted black, whereas thermostat housings were left as cast or mildly polished. The water pump and pulley should match the engine block, which was usually black. Hoses on TR4/4A cars were normally black rubber, sometimes reinforced with canvas. Fans could be silver or aluminium

The wider, smaller radiator fitted to TR4A/5/250 models, seen here on a TR5. The eight-blade yellow plastic fan and the support strut, quite different from the TR4 type, can be seen.

painted, and also black, or sometimes a combination of both.

On the six-cylinder cars, the general layout and principles of the cooling system remained similar, but the TR5/250 had an uprated radiator, even though it was outwardly similar to the TR4A item. The TR6 fielded three different radiators, which again looked similar; one was for US specification cars, the second was an early non-US type that was the same as the TR5's, and the third was the non-US type used following the change from the TR5 version. The overflow bottle system was retained for TR5/250s and TR6s, but the bottle was now located on the left-hand side of the radiator. The thermostat housing was now bolted to the top of the water pump, the thermostat itself now being fitted vertically rather than horizontally. The water pump was again belt-driven, now by a more modern V belt of thinner section, and was bolted to the front face of the cylinder head rather than to the block.

An eight-blade plastic fan was introduced, of 12½in diameter and usually coloured yellow, but sometimes black. This was bolted to the front of the crankshaft via an extension piece and was used on TR5/250s and TR6s up to engine number CP 52420HE. A seven-blade fan of similar diameter was used for the remainder of the CP series run, and for CC cars through to 1971, but 1972 US specification cars had a new 13-blade fan of 14½in diameter. CF/CR cars from the 1973 model year onwards all had this 13-blade fan, usually in red plastic although some yellow or black ones are known. The TR4A's Smiths heater unit continued virtually unchanged for the TR5/250s and TR6s, although additional vents for warming the feet and knees were incorporated. The six-cylinder cooling system was pressurised at 7psi in the later TR5/250, although the manual states that radiators on early cars were still rated at 4psi. I tend to doubt this 4psi figure, especially as the earlier TR4A had used the higher 7psi pressure. The TR6 carried a more modern high-pressure system set at 13psi – and experience has shown that 13psi suits all the six-cylinder TRs. Thermostat specification remained at 88°C (cold climate) or 82°C ('normal' climate, whatever that was). Normal running temperature remained at 185°F (85°C) and water capacity, including the heater, was 11 pints.

The colours of the cooling system components remained much as before, with the exception of the hoses. TR5s had conventional black hoses, but TR250s were given fancy ones with gold and black stripes! The 1969 model year TR6s of both types, injection and carburettor, also used these, whereas 1970 model year TR6s of both types adopted hoses in a strange moss green. These seem to have continued as standard to the end of TR6 production.

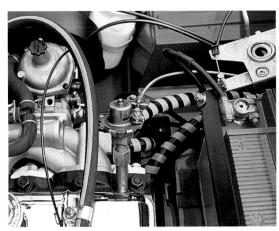

TR250s and many early carburettor TR6s sported these racy-looking black and yellow hoses. The heater control tap with its operating cable can be seen in the lower view, along with the bonnet catch assembly and cable to the right.

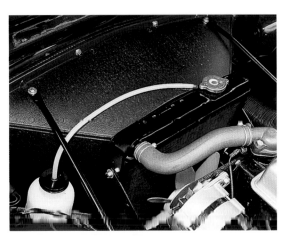

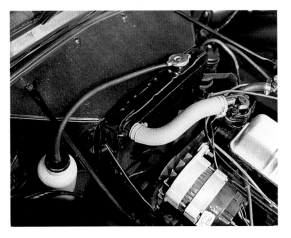

Two TR6 cooling fans. Late CP/CC series cars used a 12½in seven-blade fan (left), while late North American CC series and all CR/CF series cars had a 14½in 13-blade fan (lower left), usually in red plastic. Also visible in both views are the air deflector and the correct radiator overflow bottle and tube. The moss green colour of the cooling hoses is correct on TR6s of this period.

Exhaust System

As in so many other ways relating to the TR's mechanical hardware, the TR4 used a development of the TR3A's exhaust system, whereas the IRS cars had redesigned systems.

The exhaust system on the TR4 began as a cast unpainted four-branch manifold bolted to the cylinder head, this manifold feeding, via a flanged joint with a copper/asbestos gasket, into a single curved mild steel downpipe. The downpipe passed alongside the engine sump and very close to the inner side of the cruciform chassis bracing. It is prone to vibrate annoyingly against this unless the exhaust is carefully installed. The first mounting point was by the gearbox cross-member, and at the same point the downpipe fed into the centre section of the three-piece system, the mounting doubling as a pipe clamp. A special bracket attached the exhaust to the chassis itself. The central section contained the main silencer box, which was 24in long and of 'straight-through' design. The forward end of this section passed through the central box member of the chassis cruciform bracing to mate with the front pipe, the silencer box itself being situated just aft of the cruciform centre. The centre section joined the rear section via a pipe clamp at the rear of the main silencer, the rear section being a combined tail pipe and auxiliary 12in silencer box. The rear section had a slight crank in it, to bring the end of the tail pipe out at the rear of the car on the left-hand side looking from the rear. The second exhaust mounting was by means of a circle bracket and a reinforced rubber strap onto a bracket fixed to the rearmost of the two back chassis cross tubes.

The single tail pipe of the TR4, showing its correct, slightly upswept exit angle.

This basic type of transverse silencer, seen on a CP series TR6, was fitted to all six-cylinder cars. Blanked outlets for right-hand tail pipes can be seen, even though the exhaust always exited on the left-hand side, irrespective of steering wheel position. Note the spare wheel retaining bolt passing through the boot floor and rear chassis cross tube.

The parts catalogue shows that a tail pipe extension or finisher was specified on early TR4s, but it is not known for how long fitment of this continued. The internal diameter of the exhaust system was 1⅞in.

No changes of substance seem to have occurred to the TR4's exhaust system. When the more efficient 'TR4A' type cylinder head was brought into use on later TR4s, the equally efficient TR4A type of cast manifold with twin downpipes did not arrive with it, and thus the TR4 continued with the single downpipe system. This TR4A cast manifold was a considerable improvement, the four branches becoming two – rather than one – at the flange joint, with a new twin front pipe arrangement. This manifold was said to be worth a further 5bhp at the high end of the rev range, as gases from the inner and outer exhaust ports remained separate until they entered the front silencer box, in which they mingled to exit through a single pipe. In turn this pipe led into an elongated Y-shaped section with two exits, feeding into a pair of oval-shaped rear silencer boxes, each of which had an integral upswept tail pipe and a built-in hanger bracket. The twin tail pipes emerged under the rear bumper quite close together towards the centre of the car.

This system, with its three silencers, was not wholly satisfactory in use, as well as being costly to manufacture and replace. It certainly gave low noise levels, but did nothing for the gas flow characteristics, and rather negated the benefits from the new manifold. Consequently, a redesigned system was introduced from CTC 70489 in June 1966. The front silencer was deleted and a Y piece joining the two separate downpipes was substituted. A cranked single pipe then carried the gases to the rear of the car (passing through the chassis cruciform) into a large, single, oval-shaped, transverse silencer box with an integral tail pipe exiting on the nearside. This system was fixed as usual at the rear engine mounting, and the transverse silencer had both fore and aft flexible hangings from the chassis. Although slightly noisier, this modified exhaust was still quieter than the TR4 type and rather more efficient.

A system similar to this later TR4A type was used for the TR5, but here twin pipes were used throughout, the single transverse silencer box having twin inlets and outlets. The cast exhaust manifold was a four-branch type, two of the branches being formed of pairs of pipes to cater for the six exhaust ports. This manifold fed into a flanged joint which connected into the twin downpipes. The same exhaust manifold was used for all fuel-injected TR6s and later carburettor TR6s, but TR250s and earlier carburettor TR6s (up to car number CC 67893) had a manifold with only one exit and a single front and intermediate pipe. The transverse silencer in this case had one inlet but retained two integral tail pipes, whereas later carburettor cars and all injection TR6s had a 'twin throughout' system very similar to the TR5's. The parts books indicate several alternative silencer specifications for different export markets, notably France, Germany and Switzerland. Exhaust manifolds were left as cast, but pipes, brackets and silencers on all cars were usually finished in silver or sometimes black.

This TR6 shows the correct exit angle for the twin tail pipes used with the six-cylinder engine.

Transmission

TR gearboxes remained remarkably unaltered for many years. The unit introduced with the TR4 and 'TCF' TR3Bs was a development of the previous gearbox, differing principally in having synchromesh on first gear. As a result, the gearbox casing was ½in longer to accommodate the extra synchro cone. Although the TR2/3/3A and TR3B/4 gearboxes are interchangeable, with a little persuasion, the internals of the later unit differed considerably and ultimately proved sufficiently strong to cope with the 50% power increase of the injected six-cylinder engines.

The gearbox had a conventional H-pattern change with reverse to the right and rear. A neat remote control lever was fitted, having relatively short throws between gears. When ordered, the optional Laycock de Normanville overdrive unit was bolted direct to the rear of the gearbox casing, its place on non-overdrive cars being taken by an extended tailshaft. This arrangement allowed for easy retro-fitting of an overdrive unit or overdrive gearbox complete, as the propshaft and cross-

member did not need to be altered. The gearbox had needle roller bearings on both the mainshaft and the constant pinion shaft, and proved in service to be a particularly reliable unit. Oil capacity was 1½ pints without overdrive, 3½ pints with, the correct level being indicated by a plug on the side of the casing. The overdrive unit was operated electrically by a Lucas solenoid bolted to the side of the casing in a somewhat vulnerable position. The solenoid was actuated via two isolator switches on the top cover of the gearbox and a relay from a flick switch mounted on the steering column. The isolator switches ensured that overdrive could not be engaged in reverse or in first (second also for late TR6s). The electrical system has proved to be the Achilles heel of the overdrive transmission, most malfunctions being traceable to electrical and solenoid faults. Correct level and type of oil in the gearbox is also critical to proper and reliable operation.

When the TR gearbox was redesigned to incorporate first gear synchromesh, the linkage

This excellent view of a rebuilt TR6 rolling chassis shows the gearbox installed. Note the isolator switches on the gearbox top cover, and the rearward crank of the gear lever. The basic gearbox design remained unchanged throughout TR4-6 production.

was also slightly modified in an attempt to eliminate sloppiness and the characteristic 'buzzing' sound – familiar to sidescreen TR owners – transmitted up the gear lever under hard acceleration. However, this modification had the unfortunate effect of making the gearchange of the TR4 and subsequent TRs noticeably more notchy than that of the earlier cars, a longer gear lever being utilised to try to counteract this trait. The three upper ratios in the TR4 gearbox were similar to those of the previous unit, but first and reverse gearing was higher, giving the following internal ratios: first, 3.14; second, 2.01; second overdrive, 1.65; third, 1.33; third overdrive, 1.09; top, 1.0; top overdrive, 0.82; reverse, 3.22. This gearbox was used with only very minor modification from the TR4 of 1961 through to the early TR6s of ten years later. The parts catalogues quoted three types of gearbox and clutch housing assemblies for the TR4; up to CT 31506 (31636 overdrive), from CT 31507 (31637 overdrive) to CT 50124, and from CT 50125 onwards. The differences are minor, with interchangeability evidently not affected.

Different part numbers were also quoted for the gear lever on each model, but the chromed levers are broadly similar. A few of the earlier TR4 levers were straight, but all later TR4s and subsequent models had a lever with a slight rearwards crank. Some TR4A gear levers were shorter than others, accentuating the notchiness of the change. The TR4/4A had a round black plastic gear knob with the gate pattern cut in white, whereas standard fit for the TR5/250 was a somewhat pear-shaped item. For the TR250, the knob was trimmed in leather, but TR5 customers generally had to make do with a plastic (or hard rubber) knob, although a few TR5s also received the leather-trimmed knobs. With the introduction of the TR5/250, a rubber bush was incorporated into the knuckle/ball of the gear lever to help reduce noise transference. The 1969 model year TR6s reverted to a round plastic gear knob, this changing for 1970 (and onwards) to a pear shape again, in plastic for injection cars but fabric-trimmed for most, if not all, North American TR6s. An unspecified change in the gear knob is catalogued at car number CP 53854, but it is not certain to which change this refers.

In mid-1971, the gearbox was finally altered in substance when it received redesigned and uprated internals, developed from the stronger Triumph Stag unit. The gearbox numbers involved were CD 51163 or CC 89817 onwards. The internal ratios changed slightly, to the following: first, 2.99; second, 2.10; third, 1.39; top, 1.0; reverse, 3.37. The revised overall ratios, therefore, were: first, 10.33; second, 7.25; third, 4.78; top, 3.45; reverse, 11.62. Overall ratios were lower on North American TR6s, due to the use of

3.7:1 axle ratio. A second change to transmission specification occurred shortly after the beginning of the 1973 model year, when the old Laycock 'A' type overdrive unit (giving a step-up ratio of 0.82:1) was finally phased out after 20 years in favour of the new 'J' type. This change arrived just after the introduction of the CR series cars, it is believed at CR 567. However, it would appear that all North American specification 1973 model year cars – ie, from CF 1 onwards – with overdrive received the new 'J' type.

Although Laycock's 'J' type unit was more modern in design, it had the considerable disadvantage that it did not operate on second gear, bringing to an end the TRs unique seven-speed transmission system. The step-up ratio of this later unit was 0.797:1, so the overall gear ratio in overdrive top became 2.75:1 (based on a 3.45:1 differential), giving a road speed with standard wheels and tyres of 36.6mph per 1000rpm. With the US-specification 3.7:1 differential and the 'J' type overdrive, the overall ratio of 2.95:1 gave 26.1mph per 1000rpm, based on 185-section tyres. Finally, after 20 years in the options list, overdrive began to be standard fit on injection cars, it is thought from December 1973, at CR 5001. Overdrive remained optional on North American TR6s right to the end of production.

The gearbox and overdrive unit were finished in silver/aluminium paint or else left as cast. The propeller shaft was normally supplied by Hardy-Spicer and painted black, one shaft covering both overdrive and non-overdrive cars. A universal joint was employed at each end of the shaft, with a sliding spline joint at the forward end to allow

A correct TR4 gear lever and knob, showing the neat rubber boot fitted around the base. The carpet binding around the rubber boot is also in the correct style.

for suspension movement. On later TR6s, sealed joints were used and the grease nipples were deleted. Gearboxes were assembled in-house by Standard-Triumph, and the company also machined and hardened the gears from blanks purchased from outside sources. Overdrive units came fully assembled from Laycock Engineering, the Triumph contract being of sufficient importance to Laycock that this company had a member of staff permanently based at Triumph on troubleshooting duties.

The clutch came in for modification upon the introduction of the TR4A. The TR4 continued to use the Borg & Beck spring-type single dry-plate 9in clutch, hydraulically operated, that had been found in the sidescreen cars. However, in the interests of a lighter pedal operation, the TR4A was provided with a diaphragm spring clutch, again by Borg & Beck, but the diameter was reduced slightly to 8½in. This seems to have been a retrograde step, as more than one contemporary road test commented that clutch slip was all too easy to provoke, something to which the old spring clutch was not prone. The diaphragm clutch was self-adjusting for wear, unlike the previous type, although the TR4A retained the adjustment provision on the operating rod. Grease nipples on the clutch operating shaft mounted in the bellhousing were also deleted when the TR4A appeared. TR4 parts catalogues indicate that this diaphragm clutch was available to fit late TR4s, but only as a service replacement rather than as original equipment. Although it is believed that the diaphragm clutch only became the normal provision upon the TR4A's introduction, in January 1965, parts catalogues suggest that from August 1964 onwards it was available on TR4s as a special order, and it may indeed have been phased in gradually on some of the very last TR4s as the standard fit.

The 8½in diameter diaphragm clutch remained in use on TR5/250/6 models, but the diaphragm spring was strengthened to cope with the increased power. Correspondingly, to compensate for the increased pedal weight this would otherwise have produced, the clutch hydraulics were uprated, the system including a larger diameter slave cylinder. Some TR5/6 clutches were of Laycock manufacture, not Borg & Beck. It should be noted that Borg & Beck and Laycock clutch plates and covers must be fitted in sets (a Laycock plate will not fit a Borg & Beck cover, and *vice versa*), a fact which has caused grief to unwitting TR owners over the years. It is also essential to use the correct length of bolts for each type of clutch to avoid unpleasant problems.

Two entirely different rear axle systems were used. TR4s and the North American non-IRS TR4As had a conventional 'banjo' axle, whereas the IRS cars had the differential and crown wheel and pinion housing mounted on the chassis, with splined and jointed driveshafts driving the rear hubs and wheels.

The TR4 axle was in essence carried over from the later sidescreen cars, the only real difference being the 3in increase in track, to 48 in, achieved simply by lengthening the axle tubes and the half-shafts within. The axle was the hypoid-bevel, semi-floating type, with a detachable rear cover for access to the differential and crown wheel and pinion set. Provision was made for shim adjustment for the differential bearings and end-wise location of the crown wheel. Oil capacity was 1½ pints. The rear hubs ran on taper roller bearings and conventional oil seals were employed. At the outer ends of the axle tubes were circular flanges, to which the brake back plates were attached by six set bolts each side. This design of axle had been refined by Triumph's engineers over the 1956-60 period into a very strong unit, which has proved capable of transmitting without ill effect twice as much power as it was designed to accept. The only production modification that proved necessary during the TR4's run was a minor change in the thrust washer arrangement at axle number CT 33066. Axles were individually numbered in their own 'CT' series, and should be painted black when restored.

The standard axle ratio remained, as with the sidescreen cars, at 3.7:1, achieved by a 37-tooth crown wheel mating with a 10-tooth pinion. This ratio continued to be the standard fitting whether or not overdrive was specified, although an optional 4.1:1 axle ratio could be supplied to special order with overdrive. Cars fitted from new with the 4.1:1 axle ratio were rare, accounting for less than 10% of production I would venture to suggest. The standard 3.7:1 ratio provided almost exactly 20mph per 1000rpm in top, which increased to 24.6mph per 1000rpm in overdrive top. The 4.1:1 option gave approximately 18mph and 22mph per 1000rpm respectively. The axle used on the non-IRS TR4As was the same as the TR4 one, although there were minor differences in the spring plates and brake pipe brackets.

The IRS cars kept the same basic differential and crown wheel and pinion assembly, and on the TR4A the same two ratios were offered. The TR5 and TR6 went to a 3.45:1 ratio, for both overdrive and non-overdrive cars, but the less powerful TR250 and carburettor TR6 for the USA continued to use the original 3.7:1 ratio. The IRS type differential housing, still painted black, had mounting plates bolted to it front and rear, and on the TR4A these each carried two rubber-mounted fixings to the chassis. Owing to their extra power, the six-cylinder cars had a different rear housing cover incorporating four rear mounting points,

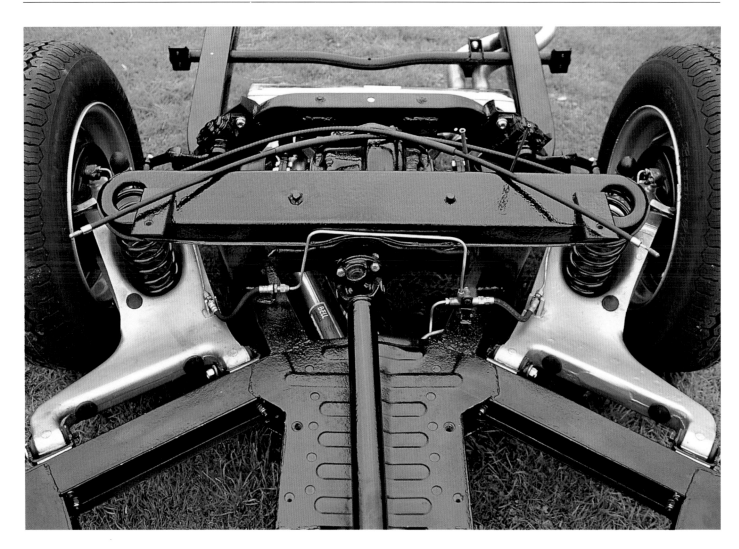

making six in all, although there still remained only four locating points on the chassis! This was possible because the two each side at the rear were connected together via mounting plates onto a single chassis mounting each side. The drive emerged from each side of the housing via short stub axles to drive flanges, to which were bolted driveshafts with universal joints at each end. The outer universal joint formed part of a further short driveshaft which fitted as a journal in a hub carrier housing bolted to the rear trailing arm. A key in the tapered driveshaft engaged with the slot and taper of the rear drive flange and hub itself. The whole rear drive unit contained so many parts, some of which needed special tools for servicing, that it is not surprising manufacturing costs increased considerably. However, the Triumph engineers, one presumes, did a thorough job when devising the IRS, as the parts catalogues show very few modifications in production. The wire wheel option, which continued to be available until 1973, necessitated hub extensions to the drive flanges.

The TR4's propshaft was marginally shorter than that of the sidescreen cars to allow for the slightly greater length of the new all-synchromesh gearbox. As previously, it was manufactured by Hardy-Spicer and painted black. Although the TR4A has two different propshafts listed (one carries the same part number as the TR4 type), I suspect that both types are in fact the same, the two part numbers merely indicating different manufacturers. The propshaft continued for the TR5 and TR6 without change, although the grease nipple was deleted in the TR6 application in respect of one of the shafts listed. The TR6 parts catalogues list the availability of 4.1.1, 4.3.1, 4.55:1 and 4.875:1 ratios for competition purposes.

The standard 3.45:1 ratio of the petrol injection cars gave the following overall gear ratios: first, 10.8:1; second, 6.92:1; third, 4.59:1; top, 3.45:1; overdrive top, 2.82:1; reverse, 11.11:1. Road speeds per 1000rpm with standard 165-section tyres were 21.2mph in top and 25.9mph in overdrive when the 'A' type overdrive was fitted. When the 'J' type overdrive replaced the 'A' type in the TR6 in 1973, road speed in overdrive became 26.6mph per 1000rpm. On North American specification cars with the 3.7:1 ratio and 185-section tyres, the 'A' type overdrive produced 25.4mph per 1000rpm and the 'J' type 26.1mph per 1000rpm.

The final drive arrangement and independent rear suspension of a TR6, but the same layout is found on TR4A/5/250 models. Clearly seen are the propeller shaft, the differential casing, the massive bridge piece holding the rear springs in place, and the cast trailing arms and their mounting arrangements. The handbrake cables, of course, are disconnected at this stage.

Chassis

Two distinct chassis types were fitted under these cars. The TR4 had a developed version of the chassis used for the sidescreen models, whereas later cars with independent rear suspension required a chassis that differed considerably. Within this latter group was also found a 'cross-breed' version which allowed live axle rear suspension to be fitted to some North American specification TR4As.

The TR4 chassis consisted of two full-length side members in 15 swg steel of roughly 3in by 3½in section, the narrower section being at the top and bottom. These two members were connected at the front by a main cross-member, and rising from the top of the side rails forward of this point were two inward-leaning towers that carried the steering rack. The front cross-member was of roughly the same section as the two side members. As compared with the sidescreen TR's very similar chassis frame, the small-diameter front cross tube was deleted for the TR4, and the two front suspension towers which encase the coil springs were repositioned slightly. These towers rose upwards from the side members at the point where the cross-member joined, and, at the top, the towers were connected to each other and prevented from collapsing inwards under suspension loads by a bolted tubular cross piece, which could be taken off to facilitate engine removal. Inner mounting points for the front suspension lower wishbones were situated either side of the suspension towers, and pointing backwards from the top of the towers were strengthening members, one on each side, which served also as additional front body mounting points. The suspension towers had pins bolted to their tops upon which the upper wishbone arms were able to pivot. Shock absorber top mounting studs also passed through the top of the towers, and box brackets carrying the rebound stops were bolted to the base of these towers.

The 49in front track of the TR4 was 4in wider than that of its predecessor, and the chassis frame was cleverly adapted to allow for this by having extra box sections welded outboard of the main chassis members at the front, effectively extending the overall width of the front of the chassis by the requisite 4in. These sections also brought the bonus of some extra stiffness to the front of the chassis. To them were welded front body mounting brackets, one each side, and at this point radiator mounting brackets were attached to the inside of the main members. A bolted radiator protection cross-piece was also fitted at the extreme front.

The main side members, which were parallel at the front, turned outwards just aft of the suspension towers to enable the chassis frame to reach its maximum width about one third of the way back, roughly in line with the top of the front bulkhead. Just past the point of maximum width, tubular body mounting outriggers were attached, passing through the main chassis members to join with the cruciform bracing that formed the central portion of the frame. There were two sets of such outriggers, the rear ones not quite as wide overall as the front ones. Body mounting plates were bolted to the top of the outriggers. Further small body mounting brackets were welded to the top of the forward part of the cruciform bracing, and the body floors bolted direct to the rear part of the cruciform. The two sides of the cruciform were connected by a central box member, through which the exhaust system passed. Just forward of this point was a bolted-in gearbox cross-member, temporary removal of which greatly facilitates gearbox extraction.

The frame narrowed towards the rear axle area, and just before the axle line upright flanged plates were welded, one to each side member, to carry the lever arm rear shock absorbers. The forward ends of the rear springs were carried on the hardened steel pins referred to in the 'Rear Suspension' section (page 94), the pins passing through the chassis. The rear axle passed over the side members, and just aft of the rear damper mountings the frame ceased to narrow and became parallel for approximately its final 3ft of length. Almost at the same point, the side members turned upwards (when seen in side view) and continued on a slight 'rising gradient' to the rear of the frame, where they were connected by two tubular cross-members of differing length. The forward one was of narrower diameter and carried the rear spring shackles at its outer ends, having

This rolling TR6 chassis, expertly restored by Dave Lewis, displays the shape of the frame better than any words can!

passed through the centre of the frame side members. The rear one, of roughly 1½in diameter, had gusset plates welded where it attached to the side members at the rear, to provide strength and rearmost body mounting points. The usual method of mounting a tow bar to a TR4 is to clamp it to these tubular members with U bolts, but it is as well to check their soundness before attempting any serious towing! Pads of insulating material were used between the body and chassis at the various mounting points.

Overall, the TR4 chassis stayed remarkably like that of the earlier TRs. The wheelbase remained the same at 88in, and it has even proved possible to fit a TR3A body onto a TR4 chassis with surprisingly little modification. As for changes to the TR4 chassis during production, the parts catalogue lists four different types of frame, although differences appear to be minor. A change occurred at CT 4387 (disc wheels) and CT 4689 (wire wheels), but it has not proved possible to ascertain exactly what this was, although it must have been associated with the steering geometry changes at the same time. At CT 20063, the front suspension towers were changed slightly, and the steering rack mountings were strengthened. At CT 23383, the changes to the rear springs detailed in the 'Rear Suspension' section (page 95) necessitated minor modification to the rear spring mounting points, and rear axle check strap mountings were

also modified at this point. Inevitably, in a production run of 40,000 cars, there were minor changes to brackets and brake and fuel pipe pick-up points, but nothing of substance.

A minor mystery surrounds the possibility of some early frames having had bolt-on side extensions to the chassis outriggers where the body mounts. No reference to these has been found in any literature, but I have heard of several cars so fitted. Examples are CT 1838L, a very original car which spent the bulk of its life in Mexico, and CT 666L, which is one of the cars illustrated in this book. Its owner, Nigel Wiggins, states that this car appears to have a modified TR3A chassis, confirmed by the fact that the tubs for mounting the rear wing struts on the TR3A are still present, although quite redundant on the TR4! It would seem that when TR4 production started, a considerable number of TR3A frames remained in stock and were suitably adapted for the new car with these outrigger extensions (to facilitate fitting the wider body) and the welded-on front extensions (to achieve the wider front track).

The chassis frame developed for the TR4A, and used with detail differences up to the TR6, was quite different since independent rear suspension necessitated a total redesign. Viewed from above, the IRS chassis has been rightly described as resembling a bell in front of an A-shaped extension, the rear legs of which form the rear chassis rails. Box-section members were again used, but ran parallel only at the extreme front. The chassis frame was very narrow at the point where the 'bell' shape met the 'A' shape, compromising torsional stiffness. Just after the point where the chassis began to widen out to the rear, a large bridge piece standing on two towers was fixed, serving as a carrier for the rear dampers and a location for the differential casing by means of two rubber-mounted rearward-facing lugs. Two further lugs located the front of the differential casing on the spring-retaining suspension bridge. A final tubular cross-member, passing through the chassis side rails, was located roughly 12in from the rear of the chassis frame, and carried exhaust hanging points. Rear body mounting points were found at the extreme end of the chassis.

Through the centre of the 'bell' passed the rear frame side members, such that for about 3ft of its length the chassis had four box-section members side by side (as viewed from above) rather than the two found for the rest of its length. The joining point under the rear of the floors was plated for strength, a hoop to accommodate the propeller shaft being added on the TR4As. Body mounting brackets were attached to the outer side members, and a bolted-in gearbox cross-member connected the two inner side members at a point a few inches aft of their join with the outer side members. Just forward of this point, the forward-facing bracing members that connected to the tops of the front suspension towers themselves met the side rails.

The front suspension towers were similar in principle and function to those of the earlier cars, but different in detail. At their base was the main box-section front cross-member. Just in front of this, steering rack mounts were welded to the chassis rails, and a bolted-in cross-tube connected the tops of the suspension towers as previously. A radiator protection shield remained and was bolted in place at the extreme front of the chassis frame. There was no longer any need for TR4-style side extension box sections at the front of the chassis, as the opportunity had been taken during the redesign to widen the distance between the front chassis rails. Body mounting brackets were fitted at the extreme front of the chassis. As detailed in the 'Front Suspension' section (page 93), the inner lower wishbone mountings were changed to brackets bolted to the side of the frame, and the top inner wishbone mountings were also modified.

This basic design of IRS chassis was also employed for the TR5/250 and TR6, with only minor differences necessitated principally by the longer six-cylinder engine. The bolted-in cross-tube was bowed somewhat to accommodate the increased engine length, while the steering rack position was also moved and the 'hoop' over the

differential area was deleted. Engine mountings, of course, were also modified.

Unfortunately, the IRS chassis proved not to be as torsionally stiff as the TR4 chassis, a fact frequently commented upon by contemporary road testers. When one views the two types of chassis together, it is not difficult to see why: with its thin 'waist' about two-thirds of the way back, the later chassis is less rigid. This relative lack of rigidity caused problems on the few IRS cars that were used in their day for rough road rallying, and probably also explains why historic rally competitors today prefer to use the TR4.

Few modifications were made to the IRS chassis frame in production, although the mounting points were modified on the six-cylinder cars to obviate problems with differentials breaking away under hard usage. The rear spring specification changes incorporated early in TR6 production at CP 52868 and CC 61571 necessitated alteration of the mounting points for the rear trailing arm brackets. TR4As onwards incorporated two front towing eyes attached to the radiator cross-piece. Restorers of IRS TRs need to pay particular attention to the condition of the rear of the chassis frame. As well as differential units breaking away, trailing arm brackets can pull through and the bridge pieces can rust badly.

I have already mentioned the curious North American specification TR4A with the TR4-type solid rear axle. This derivative, like the TR3B, was rather forced on Triumph by its US distributors, who felt that IRS represented an unnecessary complication that their customers would neither appreciate nor pay for! Thus the option of a conventionally-sprung TR4A arose just for this market – both types were sold side by side. The chassis for the live axle car was a modified TR4A type. Provision for semi-elliptic springs was made by new brackets, carrying the forward ends of the springs, being attached to the chassis rails forming the bottom of the 'bell' shape. The rear of the springs attached to conventional swinging shackles mounted on the tubular rear cross-member, very much in the style of the sidescreen cars. Dampers were still mounted on their bridge piece, but the larger bridge piece for the coil springs on IRS cars was deleted, the solid axle crossing above the chassis at this point.

Chassis frames were sourced from outside the Standard-Triumph organisation, principally from Rubery Owen and John Thompson Motor Pressings. Brochures indicated that the frames received 'thorough rust-proofing' during manufacture, but time has proved this not to have been the case. Concerning colours, most frames appear to have been black, both gloss and matt being found, although some frames painted body colour and claimed as original have been reported.

Front Suspension

The first TR4s used the same front suspension as the last TR3A/Bs, even down to geometry and spring rates; virtually all parts are interchangeable. Even the substitution of rack and pinion steering did not directly affect the suspension design. However, from commission numbers CT 4388 (disc wheels) and CT 4690 (wire wheels), new steering geometry was substituted and the top wishbones had new-style pressings with a smoother profile. Nevertheless, the basic design of the front suspension remained fundamentally unaltered right through to the TR6, with only detailed differences.

The suspension was independent, based on coil springs and upper and lower wishbones, the system deriving originally from the Triumph Mayflower saloon designed in the late '40s, although considerably strengthened over the years. The coil springs were held within the suspension towers of the chassis, telescopic shock absorbers being housed within the springs and removed from the bottom, passing through the spring pan plate that connected the two forged arms of the lower wishbone. The dampers were fixed at their tops to the suspension towers and acted, like the springs, on the lower wishbone arms. At the outer end of the top wishbone was a swivelling ball joint, bolted to a vertical link which connected the top and bottom wishbones, and carried the stub axle, brake and front wheel. The bottom of the vertical link was threaded, and this threaded portion mated with a phosphor bronze trunnion in which it was free to turn within limits, allowing for steering action. The trunnion had pins (or bolts on later cars) extending from either side and passing through bushes in the lower wishbone, allowing for the rise and fall of the suspension. These trunnions can wear rapidly, especially if not properly greased, and are the Achilles heel of the suspension design. As introduced on the TR4, the kingpin inclination was 7°, castor angle was nil, and front wheel camber (static laden) was 2°. The inner ends of the wishbones pivoted on bronze/nylon bushes which attached to the chassis by brackets and pins at the bottom, and were carried at the top on a pin bolted to the top of the suspension tower. By

modern standards, the front suspension design is complex, its many wearing parts making overhaul relatively expensive and time-consuming.

Although the overall length of the shock absorbers varied slightly from time to time, this does not appear to have affected interchangeability in pairs. Woodhead Monroe or Armstrong

High view of the front suspension, here on a TR6, shows the double wishbone layout. The anti-roll bar fitted as standard to these cars can be seen at the bottom.

Side view shows the bronze trunnion (below the brake caliper) and coil spring with telescopic shock absorber within. The two holes in the chassis strut running to the top of the spring tower are for body mounting bolts.

usually provided the original equipment dampers, several different specifications being tried over the years, including a type specified for the USA only. Many different types of adjustable shock absorbers are available for TR4-6 models today, and fitting these can greatly improve roadholding. Adjustable front shock absorbers, of unknown type, were available from Triumph to special order during the '60s. Damper colour is one area where one cannot be categorical, many different hues having been used. If in doubt, however, black could not be considered wrong.

Following the changes referred to above at CT 4388 (disc wheels) and CT 4690 (wire wheels), further modifications were incorporated shortly thereafter, at CT 6344 (disc wheels) and CT 6389 (wire wheels). Different upper wishbones and ball joints were fitted, and the steering tie rod levers and bottom trunnions were altered. The castor angle was adjusted to 3° to aid steering self-centring at speed. This caused the trunnions to become 'handed', whereas they had previously been universal. Trunnion to lower wishbone grease seals were modified at CT 7218. The front coil springs were lengthened at CT 29984, allowing the large packing pieces that had been sited

above the springs to be deleted. Ignorance about the two types of front spring and the use of packing pieces has led to puzzlement among home mechanics, who have wondered at the eccentric front ride heights of their TR4s!

Upon the introduction of the TR4A, a significant – and unfortunate in retrospect – modification was made to the front lower wishbone inner fulcrum points. Whereas the TR4 had used the proven TR3 type with pivot pins forming part of the chassis, for the TR4A and later cars, which were deemed to require a raised front roll centre to complement the new independent rear end, a simple bracket, bolt and bush arrangement was employed as the lower inner wishbone fulcrum point both for the front and rear attachments. These brackets were bolted to the front chassis rails, with one bolt for the TR4A but two for the six-cylinder cars. While the system had the required effect on the roll centre, it proved in later years to be vulnerable to the bolts pulling straight out of a chassis weakened by rust and fatigue – or even to the chassis itself fracturing – with alarming and potentially fatal consequences. The use of wider wheels and tyres over the years has accentuated this tendency, but strengthened parts are now available. Any TR4A/5/250/6 owner should examine this area regularly. The attachment of the trunnion to the lower wishbone was also altered, becoming a bolt fixing rather than the pins protruding from the trunnion as previously.

As with the TR4, the TR4A used different types of front coil springs, some with packing pieces. Careful study of the parts catalogue is necessary to obtain correct ride height. TR5/250s had mildly uprated coil springs to handle the increased weight and power of the six-cylinder engine, but in other respects the TR4A front suspension was unaltered. For the TR6, however, an anti-roll bar at last became standard. It was attached to the lower wishbones by a drop link and to the front of the chassis frame by U bolts and brackets. The anti-roll bar had been an option on the TR4, but some doubt exists as to whether it continued to be available for the TR4A/5/250. It does not seem to have been specifically listed as an option, but I believe it was available in practice and that quite a number of cars were fitted with it from new. Yet again, front springs and shock absorbers of differing rates were employed for the TR6. In particular, the US carburettor car's front springs differed from those of the injected cars. In other respects however, both types of TR6 continued to employ the same basic front suspension as had been in use on the earlier cars.

Front suspension components should, as a general rule, be painted black or, as in the case of ball joints and trunnions, be left in their natural metal finish.

Rear Suspension

Two very different types of rear springing are found on these cars. The TR4 has a system that is, except for small detailed differences, the same as that fitted to the sidescreen cars. Even the rates of the springs initially remained the same, although the springing effectively became softer because the TR4 was roughly 70lb heavier at the rear.

The TR4's rear suspension could hardly be simpler, comprising two semi-elliptic 'cart' springs bolted to an axle, with no further location! The rear axle passed over the chassis frame, which restricted wheel movement in a downward direction. The springs were stiff to assist with axle location, and were composed of six leaves, clipped together fore and aft and having a nominal laden camber of ⅛in negative, static deflection being quoted as 4in. Metal check strap hoops were bolted over the axle to restrict upwards movement, and rubber bump stops with both an upper and lower face were wired around the axle to engage with the check straps and the top face of the chassis. The restricted wheel movement allowed by this suspension ensured that the TR4 continued to enjoy the sidescreen car's reputation for harsh and uncomfortable rear springing combined with somewhat erratic rear-end roadholding – but moderate compensation was simplicity and cheapness of maintenance! At their forward ends the springs were anchored on removable pins mounted through the chassis frame side members. These pins should draw out towards the centre of the car to facilitate easy spring removal, but they are frequently seized in position, requiring heat and much hammering to remove them. At their rear ends, the springs were mounted on shackles which swung to allow for spring deflection. Rubber bushing was fitted to the shackles, and the forward end spring bush was of the 'metalastic' type. Springs were attached to the axle by U bolts and bottom plates, to which the lever arm Armstrong shock absorbers were also connected by rubber-bushed links. The dampers themselves

The live axle rear suspension of the TR4, showing the semi-elliptic spring, the hoop that restrains upward movement of the axle, and the lever arm shock absorber. Bolt-on wire wheel hub extensions are fitted to this car. The silver paint finish (as opposed to black) of the brake drum is debatable as regards originality.

Comparable TR4A view of the independent rear suspension, showing the coil spring, transversely mounted lever arm shock absorber, trailing arm and bump stop. The driveshaft can also be discerned.

The independent rear suspension on display with body removed, seen from front and rear. Interesting features are the cast alloy semi-trailing arm, shock absorber link, driveshaft arrangement and handbrake cable run.

were bolted to brackets which formed part of the chassis frame. Uprated competition springs were available for TR4s, usually having further leaves in addition to a full-length second leaf below the main top leaf. Although these springs achieved their designed purpose, use of competition springs on a normal road car can lead to unacceptable rear end harshness, and should only be fitted after careful consideration.

Several changes in the rear suspension specification took place during the life of the TR4, starting at CT 2829, when two identical rear springs were fitted, whereas previously they had had differing rates. Rear springs were changed again at CT 23383, the 'deep-dished' type of spring being introduced with aluminium packing between the spring and axle. The rear axle check strap was modified, and the spring 'eye-to-eye' distance was reduced, necessitating a minor chassis change. Rear shock absorbers were modified at CT 3434 and again at CT 11479, the last type being common with those then in use on the TR3B. After the change at CT 3434, a different specification of rear shock absorber was utilised for US-bound cars.

The arrival of the TR4A in March 1965 introduced independent rear suspension in conjunction with the redesigned chassis frame described earlier (pages 90-91), the principles of the IRS being borrowed from the Triumph 2000 saloon that had been introduced 18 months previously. This suspension continued to the end of TR6 production, with limited modification.

The rear wheels were carried on large cast alloy semi-trailing 'wishbones', each pivoted on bolts and bushes running in backwards-facing brackets (two on each side) fixed to the chassis frame. Shims were interposed at the attachment points to provide for adjusting wheel alignment and camber. A single coil spring on each side bore on the trailing arm's upper face at its lower end, and was restrained at its top end by a large transverse chassis bridge piece. A rubber seating ring was inserted above the coil spring to insulate the chassis from high-frequency road vibration. A conical rubber bump stop was fitted to the underside of the body on each side, bearing on the arm itself in full-bump conditions. Lever arm shock absorbers were mounted laterally, and at a 45° angle, on a second bridge piece which also formed a chassis cross-member. The arms of the dampers were connected to the trailing edge of the trailing arm by rubber-bushed drop links.

This 'trailing arm wishbone' design was a great advance on the Herald type of swing axle IRS, and had the virtue of avoiding the violent camber changes to which cheaper forms of IRS are prone. The rear suspension, however, did turn out to be rather soft compared with earlier TRs – tail squat under acceleration was a particular feature of all independently sprung TRs. Under static unladen conditions, a slight positive camber of around 1° was built into the suspension, but this could be seen to change to negative camber under heavy loads or cornering forces. Vertical wheel movement, of course, was considerably greater than with the TR3A/4 design, with a consequent increase in comfort and roadholding, albeit at the price of more complexity and expense. Ground clearance remained the same as the TR4 at 6in.

Two modifications were incorporated into the rear suspension during the TR4A's run, the first very soon after the car's introduction. At CTC 52387, the rear bump stop rubbers were extended because it had been found that extreme conditions of bump could make the trailing arm contact the rear brake hose and possibly damage it. This modification was hopefully retro-fitted to all earlier TR4As, although possibly some escaped. Later in the run, at CTC 69746, revised rear springs of increased length were introduced to counteract what was said to be a 'heavy knock' in the rear suspension.

On the TR5/250 stiffer rear springs were used to deal with the increased power, although rear shock absorbers were the same as on the TR4A. The bump stops were moved from the body to the trailing arm itself, but the rebound stop continued to act on the arm of the damper. The repositioning of the bump stop involved recasting the trailing arm, resulting in many detailed differences although the two types looked similar. The TR4A type had a 'dish' for the bump stop impact (the rubber stop was mounted on the body turret), whereas the TR5 type had a 'tower' for bump stop mounting (the rubber stop impacted on the body turret). Somewhat surprisingly, the shock absorbers remained unchanged – and continued as standard specification for the TR6 although uprated dampers were available. The TR6 at first used the same coil springs as the TR5, but from CP 52868 and CC 61571 these were uprated and the trailing wishbone arm support brackets were strengthened. Uprated springs would have meant a change in ride height and camber, so the brackets received altered pivot and location holes to restore ride height and camber to former levels. In other respects, the IRS system continued virtually unchanged to the end of TR6 production.

Mention has been made in the 'Chassis' section (page 91) of the solid axle TR4A offered in North America. This variant used a conventional TR4 axle suspended on equally conventional semi-elliptic springs. However, the TR4A's IRS chassis was used, with special brackets to carry the forward end of the springs. The rear of the springs rode on swinging shackles attached to the rear chassis cross-tube, which thus once again fulfilled a vital part of its original function. Lever arm shock absorbers were mounted as on the IRS TR4A, these acting via 90° drop links on the distance pieces which were sited above the springs and clamped to them by U bolts.

Because the cars fitted with solid axle rear suspension were numbered in the normal TR4A commission number series, albeit with a TR4 'CT' prefix rather than a TR4A 'CTC' one, it has not proved possible to establish exactly how many were made. Only study of the entire run of build records for all cars between CTC 50001 and CTC 78687, a major task, could establish this for certain. However, it seems likely that about one in three of the TR4As sold in North America had the live axle, so around 7000 or so were made. By late 1967, one assumes that the North American market must have absorbed the idea of independent rear suspension, as no such solid axle 'option' was offered for the TR250.

Concerning colours, rear springs were usually left in natural metal, although both leaf and coil springs could not be criticised if painted black. Lever arm dampers seem to have been painted black or silver, or left natural. Some after-market replacements come in colours that are verging on the garish, and would perhaps be better refinished in black.

Steering

The arrival of the TR4 saw a major advance in the steering system fitted to TRs, as a rack and pinion mechanism was utilised for the first time. Manufactured by Alford and Alder, this endowed the TR4 and subsequent models with light, accurate and positive steering – quite a contrast from the heavy and vague steering that was arguably the worst feature of the sidescreen cars. The great majority of all these TRs were left-hand drive.

The rack was mounted behind the radiator and ran transversely above the chassis frame members, attached by U bolts to brackets welded to the top of the chassis. From the rack, ball-jointed track rod ends bolted to steering levers, which were in turn bolted to the vertical links forming part of the front suspension. Rubber bellows were wired in place at each end of the rack to exclude dust and retain lubricant, and track adjustment was effected by lock-nutted and threaded ends on the steering rack tie rods. Steering lock stop setting remained by means of a bolt and collar adjustment on the vertical link and trunnion.

The steering column, incorporating two flexible couplings, was in three basic pieces: an upper inner and upper outer column together with a lower column which fed into the rack. Splined clamps and 'flats' on the column allowed for some measure of in/out adjustment, and there was a modicum of 'collapsible' crash protection compared with the sidescreen TR column, which could be lethal in the event of a frontal impact. The TR4A was described in sales literature as having a 'collapsible' steering column, whereas that on the TR250 was given the snappy title of 'Impactoscopic'. To justify this, a steering rack 'impact stop' was fitted on the left-hand side of the TR250's chassis to prevent the column being pushed back towards the driver, this therefore only proving effective on left-hand drive cars. The 'impact stop' was apparently still in the same position on right-hand drive TR5s, but as it was redundant the 'Impactoscopic' reference was absent from TR5 literature. Why drivers of right-hand drive TR5s did not merit equal protection is unknown. The impact absorber was present on all types of TR6, irrespective of the steering side.

Two types of rack were used on the TR4, the

The steering rack bellows and track rod end can be glimpsed in this view of a TR4 with the front wheel removed.

change taking place at CT 20064 (LHD) and CT 20266 (RHD). At this point, the previous solid aluminium block mountings were changed to rubber bushes, and the steering arms and chassis mounts differed. The specification of the rack mounting rubber bushes changed at CT 29156 to a firmer type. In November 1965, during TR4A production, a nylon spring-loaded plunger was introduced to bear on the steering rack in an attempt to counteract rattles and vibration being transferred to the steering wheel. Factory instructions were issued for the retro-fitting of this plunger to the racks of any earlier cars that had suffered the problem. The later type of TR4 rack continued for all subsequent models.

Discrepancies in the number of turns from lock to lock, and in the turning circle, are apparent from various published sources of information. The TR4 is quoted variously as having a turning circle of 31, 32 or 33ft, the number of turns from lock to lock being given as 2½, 2⅔ or 2¾. One late sales brochure quotes 3¼ turns for the TR4, and it is probable that some late TR4s had the TR4A steering rack. What is clear, however, is that all TR4As did have lower geared steering, presumably in an effort to lighten the action further. The accepted figure for the TR4A is 3½ turns, this coming down to 3¼ turns for the TR5/250 and

TR6. As the rack was unchanged for the six-cylinder cars, one presumes that the lock-stop settings were amended to take account of the wider wheels being fitted. Various figures were also quoted for the turning circle, the TR4A owners' handbook giving 30ft, whereas the workshop manual stated 33ft and some sales brochures quoted 34ft – yet all these were official factory publications! The TR250 was stated to have a 33ft turning circle, and, assuming that this is correct, the TR5 figure must be very similar. On the TR6, official literature quoted 34¾ft left and 35½ft right.

On the TR4 front wheel toe-in was ⅛in, camber angle was 2°, castor angle was 3° and swivel pin inclination was 7°. As mentioned in the 'Front Suspension' section (page 92), the earliest TR4s had nil castor angle, but were otherwise the same. The TR4A and TR5/250 had front wheel toe-in of 0-¹⁄₁₆in, camber angle of ½°, castor angle of 2¾° and swivel pin inclination of 8½°. The TR6 had the same toe-in, camber and castor values, but the swivel pin inclination was 9°.

The standard TR4 steering wheel was a 16in Bluemels in black plastic with three spokes, the spokes each consisting of four wires disposed in a T shape. The central horn push usually, but not always, carried a 'Triumph' shield badge. The TR4A used a similar wheel, but replacement of standard steering wheels by fancy after-market ones over the years means that original TR4/4A wheels in good condition are now hard to find. Even harder to find, should it have been replaced, is the original TR5/250 15in steering wheel, which was unique to this model. Having the

spokes and rim covered with foam-filled matt black material, vinyl for the spokes and leather for the rim, succeeded in giving a more up-to-date appearance. The Triumph-badged central horn push was still used.

Upon introduction, the TR6 had a black 15in steering wheel with non-padded spokes, each spoke having holes of increasing diameter towards the centre, while the padded hub contained six visible bolts around its perimeter. The Triumph shield was retained. This type of wheel was short-lived, as cars from the 1970 model year (CP 50001 onwards) had a wheel with a silver anodised finish and spokes with slots, not holes. US-specification 1970 model year cars from CC 50001 also had a slotted wheel, but it had a black anodised finish instead of silver. The arrival of the CR series TR6s at the end of 1972 brought a new 14½in steering wheel with slightly thicker rim padding, central boss padding with fake stitching instead of the previous smooth finish, and white 'Triumph' lettering on the horn push.

The introduction of a steering lock to the TR range was progressive. As far back as late TR4s and all TR4As, cars for Germany (and possibly Switzerland) had one as standard. The TR5 had a lock as standard for several European countries. The North American TR250s and carburettor TR6s of the 1969 model year had the option of a lock, although it seems that most cars had one fitted. A steering lock became standard on carburettor TR6s from CC 50001 and left-hand drive injection cars from CP 50001, but home market TR6s had to wait until early in 1971, at CP 52786.

Steering wheel evolution, from top left. 1) The correct TR4/4A 16in Bluemels wheel had wired spokes and a plastic rim. 2) TR5/250 models had a unique 15in wheel, with foam-backed vinyl on the spokes and a stitched leather rim. 3) TR6s for the 1969 model year only had a 15in wheel with non-padded spokes drilled with holes in which fingers could get stuck. 4) For CP series TR6s from the 1970 model year, the spokes of the 15in wheel contained tapered slots rather than holes, and a smooth surface for the hub. 5) The wheel for North American CC series TR6s from the 1970 model year was the same design, but the anodised finish of the spokes was black rather than silver. 6) Late TR6s of the CR/CF series had a slightly smaller wheel, of 14½in diameter, with fake stitching on the hub and 'Triumph' lettering.

Brakes

In late 1956 the TR3 became the world's first mass-produced car to feature disc brakes as standard equipment, these greatly improving both stopping power and fade resistance. The TR3/3A front brake system was gradually modified and refined through the late '50s, and in 1961 the late TR3A disc brake set, of Girling manufacture, was considered wholly adequate to graft onto the heavier TR4 with virtually no modifications.

The front discs were of 11in diameter, the Girling calipers being of the 'B' type, assembled in two halves (unlike earlier ones) for ease of servicing. The calipers were carried on substantial brackets attached to the front suspension vertical links, and dust shields were also incorporated. Four bolts secured the discs direct to the front hubs, the braking assembly remaining the same whether or not wire wheels were specified. Rear drum brakes were of 9in diameter by 1¼in width, a single wheel cylinder of ¾in bore operating each pair of linings. The wheel cylinder slid in the brake back plate within limits to allow for handbrake operation. A total of 88½sq in of friction lining (28sq in front, 60½sq in rear) worked on a rubbed area of disc and drum combined of 346sq in. Pendant pedals, fitted with grip rubbers and acting directly on the master cylinder via a pedal box, were fitted to all models. Separate master cylinders, each with its own fluid reservoir, were used for brake and clutch systems.

A single brake pipe carried the hydraulic action to the rear brakes, the movement of the rear axle being allowed for by a single flexible pipe. Rigid brake pipes passed along the axle to each wheel cylinder and had enough 'give' to take account of the sliding movement of the rear wheel cylinders. Each front brake was operated via a flexible hose screwed into the caliper at one end, and mounted on a chassis bracket near the suspension tower at the other. Conventional steel brake pipes and brass connectors linked the flexible hoses with the master cylinder. Rear brakes were adjusted by an inward/outward screw protruding through the back plate, and operating wedges and tappets bearing on the shoes. This type of adjuster is unfortunately very prone to seizure. Disc brakes are, of course, self-adjusting.

The mechanical handbrake of the TR4 operated on both rear wheels, and has always been most efficient if kept in good order – it is fully capable of locking the rear wheels at 30mph! This efficiency is largely due to the tremendous mechanical advantage available from the length of the lever, which was fitted with a racing-style fly-off action and locking button which is guaranteed to confuse youthful MoT testers nowadays! The handbrake grip, a push fit on to the top of the lever, was usually moulded from black plastic, although other colours occur occasionally. The lever itself and its locking button were chromed, the black rubber sealing boot at its base was screwed to the floor, and the quadrant-style ratchet mechanism was positioned directly below this point. A single sheathed cable connected to the lever pulled on a compensating bell-crank assembly mounted on a bracket on the rear axle, and, from here, open cables ran to the back of each brake drum. These engaged with a lever that passed through each brake back plate and caused the wheel cylinder to slide and mechanical expanders to apply the shoes to the drums. One peculiarity of the handbrake is that the lever was

The brake and clutch master cylinders, with their reservoirs, are seen in this view of an early TR4. The indirect-acting servo was an optional extra. A warning flag has been attached to the brake reservoir – possibly concerning silicon fluid?

always fitted on the right-hand side of the transmission tunnel, irrespective of steering position. Drivers of right-hand drive TR4s will be familiar with the constant rubbing of the left leg against the handbrake!

Several modifications to the TR4 braking system occurred early in production. From CT 4388 (disc wheels) and CT 4690 (wire wheels), completely different Girling disc calipers were fitted, of type 16P. Pad size was reduced, and the diameter of the discs themselves was also slightly reduced. The swept area of the new pads was only 20.7sq in. For an unknown reason, pads were changed again at CT 7630 (wire wheels) and CT 7747 (disc wheels). At CT 5782 (disc wheels) and CT 5855 (wire wheels) the bore of the brake master cylinder changed from 0.75in to 0.70in, the type respectively indicated by having one or two rings cast into the circumference of the cylinder body. Around the same time, at CT 5656 (wire wheels) and CT 5783 (disc wheels), the bore diameter of the rear wheel slave cylinders was reduced to 0.70in, apparently to soften the brake pedal action following the earlier caliper change. Clearly, a good deal of experimentation with brake specification went on during the early TR4 period. One further change, to the method of operation of the brake lights, took place from CT 26930. Up to this point, the brake lights had been activated by a hydraulic switch in the brake pressure line, but from this car, and for all later TRs, a spring plunger switch operating directly on the brake pedal mechanism was substituted. This necessitated a slight change in the master cylinder support bracket to provide a mounting for the new switch.

The TR4A used the front braking system – pads, discs and calipers – from late TR4s. The internals and dimensions of the rear brakes were also similar, but a different drum was used on the TR4A owing to the hub changes necessitated by IRS. The TR4A's handbrake system (including that on the North American solid axle cars) was quite new – and, as anyone who has had to stop with the handbrake will confirm, vastly inferior. One must presume that it was redesigned not only because of the arrival of IRS, but also to solve the old problem of the lever having to be on the right-hand side of the transmission tunnel, regardless of steering wheel position. The new handbrake lever, which sat on top of the tunnel, was not as long as the old one, and this, combined with the higher mounting position, ensured that much less 'pull' could be exerted. A fly-off action, as on the TR4, was initially retained, but deleted for the TR5/250/6. A fork piece at the base of the lever pulled via a compensator on to twin cables, these each comprising an inner and an outer cable. These cables ran directly via fork ends to the brake

levers on the rear brake back plates, travelling on top of the spring-retaining chassis bridge piece and along the rear trailing arms. This handbrake design continued through to the end of the TR6.

The TR4A's discs and 16P calipers were considered adequate for the TR5/250 and TR6, so the rear brakes also continued virtually unchanged on these models. However, upon the introduction of the TR5/250, a brake servo became standard for the first time. During TR4/4A production, it had been possible to order a servo as an option, that supplied being of the indirect acting type. The TR5/250 servo was of the direct acting type, and

TR4's Girling front disc braking seen in early (top) and late (above) forms. Caliper (and pad) size was obviously reduced for the later cars, but the discs themselves were also slightly smaller. After this change, the disc brakes continued with relatively few alterations through to the end of TR6 production.

A Girling warning transfer to original style, although this one is a reproduction.

The TR4 handbrake was always mounted on the right-hand side of the transmission tunnel, regardless of steering wheel position. Rubber mats are the correct floor covering for earlier TR4s, and the coarse pile carpet is accurate for the earlier cars.

The handbrake on TR4A/5/250/6 models was mounted on the transmission tunnel within a vinyl gaiter, as seen on a late TR6 to North American specification.

changed sides, along with the pedal box and new tandem master cylinder, for left-hand or right-hand drive. There was a modern, translucent plastic brake fluid reservoir with a large diameter cap, and both the pedal box and brake pedal itself differed from the TR4A. The servo could be of either Motavac or Powerstop manufacture in the case of the optional TR4/4A unit, but the TR5/250/6 servo was made by Girling. The new tandem master cylinder operated the front and rear brakes independently as a safety feature, this arrangement continuing on the TR6. TR250s and, apparently, some left-hand drive TR5s had a dashboard warning light which was illuminated by a pressure differential sensor if one of the two circuits failed, thus alerting the driver. This arrangement was also found on North American TR6s and on TR6 PIs for certain European markets – one presumes its presence depended on local legislation. UK drivers were presumably supposed to know when half their brakes had failed...

During 1969, a new caliper known as type 16PB was introduced for the TR6. It was completely interchangeable with the old 16P type, and evidently there are cases of TR6s being built with a 16PB caliper on one side and a 16P on the other! During the TR6 production run, anti-rattle springs were introduced for the disc pads from mid-1972, and the thread on the caliper assemblies was changed from Imperial to Metric at CP 76095 and CC 81079, but otherwise there were no significant braking modifications.

While the TR4 brake system had only three flexible hydraulic pipes, the IRS cars needed four. The rear brakes had one each, connected by a transverse pipe that crossed the chassis on the spring-retaining bridge piece. Additional rigid brake piping was necessary on TR5/250/6s to cope with the separated front and rear brake circuits and tandem master cylinder arrangement. The North American specification rigid-axle TR4A needed only three flexible pipes, one for each front wheel and a single rear one from the chassis to the left-hand brake back plate. From here, a rigid pipe traversed the axle to activate the other rear brake. This model, however, did have the TR4A handbrake arrangement with twin cables.

Brake drums on most cars were painted black, but some silver-painted ones are claimed as original on wire-wheeled cars. Calipers were either painted black or left as cast. Master and slave cylinders were usually left in their natural metal finish. Disc dust shields were also painted black.

Apart from the servo option on the TR4/4A, the only other brake system option available was that of 'Al-fin' drums for the TR4 rear brakes. Made of cast aluminium with steel liners, these drums offered better brake cooling properties, but they were expensive and are rarely seen.

Wheels & Tyres

As standard, the TR4 and TR4A both used the same 15in 4½J disc road wheels, chromed nave plates and 'globe' medallions as the later sidescreen cars. The medallions were the painted type with longitude bars in relief, rather than the smooth vitreous-enamelled alternative. Disc wheels were finished in silver lacquer or aluminium wheel paint.

As usual, wire wheels were optionally available. Early TR4 customers received only 48-spoke wires (with 4in rims), which were inadequate for the weight and speed of the car. This was the optional wire wheel that had been used on the TR2/3/3A, but the availability of a stronger 60-spoke alternative (with 4½J rims) on later versions of those cars makes it surprising that early TR4s had to make do with the 48-spoke version. It is not certain how many such cars were supplied. Certainly a late 1962 brochure refers to optional wire wheels as having 60 spokes, and it may be that both 60-spoke and 48-spoke wheels were sold alongside each other for a period in 1961-62. It

would be unwise today to use original 48-spoke wheels for anything other than 'show' purposes or very gentle motoring. Once it had become the norm, the 60-spoke wheel continued unchanged through TR4/4A production and into the TR5/250 era. It has been contended that TR5/250s were given 5J wire wheels, but this is probably incorrect as the parts catalogue lists the same part number for both the TR4A and TR5/250 wire wheel, and it would seem that even the TR250, which had wider tyres than the TR5, still came with 4½J wire wheels. Chromed knock-off nuts were normally fitted to TR4/4A wire wheels, but octagonal safety nuts, supplied with a large spanner for removal, were standard for some markets from the start of TR4 production. Germany, Austria and Switzerland, for instance, received cars with octagonal nuts. Finishes available for wire wheels were lacquer paint (aluminium or silver) or chrome (bright or dull), although the parts catalogue indicates that silver lacquer and dull chrome were deleted for the TR5/250.

The traditional Triumph 'Globe' motif, seen here in the painted version with lines of latitude and longitude in relief, featured on the chromed nave plates of TR4/4A disc wheels, which are now rarely seen. The British Isles appear disproportionately large! The motif is secured to the nave plate by a small nut and washer.

The standard TR4/4A/5/250 wire wheel (opposite left) had 60 double-butted spokes, although some of the earliest TR4s had the old 48-spoke variety, which was inadequate for the weight of the car. This TR4 wheel, with the correct 'eared' hub nuts, is in the painted and lacquered finish more commonly found at the time, whereas today many restorers prefer to fit chromed wheels. Optional 60-spoke painted wire wheels seen on a TR250 (opposite right), complete with the octagonal 'safety' hub nut specified for these and later models. Red-band tyres of 185 section were commonly, although not invariably, fitted to TR250s, as well as to many US-specification TR6s. Chromed wire wheels with 72 spokes and 5½J section were available as an option on the TR6 (below left),

although with an octagonal 'safety' hub nut. This example is fitted to a TR4, which makes the car look good but is not of the correct period. Rarely seen nowadays are the 'Rostyle' wheel trims (below right) fitted as standard to TR5/250s and 1969 model year TR6s. These trims, which were merely a push-fit on to the wheel, frequently flew off, often when the car hit a bump at speed. The five wheel nuts are dummies. Standard CP/CC series TR6 wheels (bottom left) had a black-finished centre and a red 'TR6' motif. For CR/CF series TR6s the wheels received satin silver centres (bottom right). On these later wheels the rim was welded to the centre all round, not just at specific points. This wheel also has the polished rim finisher commonly fitted to US-specification TR6s.

Close-up of the 'eared' knock-off hub nut used for most markets on TR4/4A models with wire wheels. As these are naturally 'handed' left and right, fitting them – and their corresponding splined hubs – on the wrong side of a car will lead to inevitable and rapid wheel loss! Only the removal instructions, not the manufacturer's name, appeared on the nut.

The rim width of the standard disc wheels for the TR5/250 increased to 5J. To enable the spare wheel to fit its compartment easily, the load board above the wheel was raised slightly – a much easier solution than increasing the depth of the spare wheel well pressing. TR5/TR250 disc wheels were equipped with 'Rostyle' wheel trims of the type fashionable in the late '60s, but these look more than somewhat dated today. Their appearance was a combination of matt black and stainless steel, with five spokes and five fake wheel nuts. These items have a reputation for falling off the wheels and visiting the scenery when a car hits a bump at speed, and original ones are not easy to find in good condition. Wheel finish below the 'Rostyle' cover continued to be silver lacquer or aluminium paint.

A further increase in rim width was provided for TR6 disc wheels, which were 5½J. The Rostyle trims of 1969 model year TR6s were fitted with slightly extended 'pips' to hold them in place. From CP 50001, a new disc wheel design was introduced, with 15 instead of 12 radial cooling holes and a matt black hub trim that left the four wheel nuts – now domed and chrome-plated – exposed. The redundant holding 'pips' for the Rostyle trims were deleted, while in the centre of the hub trim was a red badge with 'TR6' written in white. Upon the introduction of the CR series TR6s at the end of 1972, the hub centre trims on the disc wheels changed from matt black to a satin silver finish. Later American specification TR6s wore deep rim embellishers, made from highly polished brushed aluminium or sometimes stainless steel. These became standard on carburettor TR6s from 1971, but they were never offered on new injection TR6s, even as an option. However, they could be purchased as an after-market fitting from UK dealers, so they are sometimes seen on home market TR6s.

A wire wheel option – using a stronger 5½J rim with 72 spokes – remained for the TR6 until May 1973, but it became increasingly less popular during the car's production, leading to its deletion at that date. However, a number of TR6s, and TR4/4A/5/250s as well, have been retro-fitted with wire wheels of varying types. This conversion is very straightforward, it being necessary simply to bolt on splined hub extensions to carry the wire wheels, having first shortened the wheel studs to provide clearance. The finish of TR6 wire wheels as factory supplied was either bright chrome or zinc-plated silver. Octagonal safety nuts were used for all markets.

A 6J cast alloy spoked wheel was available for TR4As and TR5/250s as an extra cost option. This bolt-on wheel, which is extremely rare, carried part number 308304. It is mentioned in the relevant parts catalogues, but a service note I have seen refers to its deletion from October 1968. It has not proved possible to find an example for photography for this book.

Another possible option concerns the listing of 14in diameter wheels for TR4/4As. This size is referred to in a couple of places in Triumph literature, but it may simply be a mistake. Alternatively, it has been suggested that such wheels may have had an application for racing in the USA, where an 'option' had only to be listed by the manufacturer to be eligible for use on racing TRs, whether or not that option was genuinely available to the public! Further evidence concerning 14in TR wheels is awaited…

The TR4 came as standard on the 5.50-15 or 5.90-15 cross-ply Dunlop tyres that had been supplied for TR3As. Dunlop RS5 high-speed tyres, Michelin X radials and Goodyear white-wall tyres were optional extras. Later in the production run, Goodyear 'Motorway Special' tyres were also offered – and occasional supply problems led to other brands being used.

The TR4A was introduced with cross-ply tyres as standard, but it seems that most cars were actually delivered on radials of various types, at least for the home market. The cross-ply tyres were initially listed as 5.90-15 size, but an early sales brochure refers to the size as 6.95-15. For the USA, where radial-ply tyres were slower to catch on, Goodyear 'Grand Prix' cross-plies in 6.95-15 section were usually supplied, these being described in sales brochures as tyres of 'semi-racing construction'. Dunlop SP41 and Michelin X radials, together with various white-wall tyres, were offered as options for all markets, the radial tyres being of 165 section.

As far as I can ascertain, all TR5s, whether on disc or wire wheels, were delivered on 165-section radial tyres, either Dunlop SP41s or Michelins of the then new and revolutionary asymmetrical XAS pattern. TR250s appear always to have had fatter tyres of 185 section. As the car was considerably slower than the injected TR5, this seems to have been more of a marketing ploy than a necessity. Such tyres were also usually of the 'red-band' type – Goodyear G800 or Michelin Red Line – then fashionable in North America. TR250 catalogues state that red-band tyres were standard, but some cars are believed to have been supplied with conventional all-black rubber.

Original tyres for the injected TR6, with disc or wire wheels, were 165HR15 radials of Goodyear, Dunlop or Michelin XAS brands. As with the TR250, North American TR6s had 185-section tyres. It is believed that some European market TR6s went out on 175-section Michelin XAS tyres, and also that some later TR6s supplied to markets other than North America also had 185-section tyres from new.

TR4 'GTR4 Dove'

The only serious attempt to provide different coachwork on the TR4/4A chassis was made in 1963 by a South London Triumph dealer and TR specialist, L.F. Dove and Co of Wimbledon. This firm perceived a market for a closed coupé version of the TR4 that would provide good weather protection, a pair of moderately practical rear seats for children or small adults, and an improved luggage area accessed by an opening tailgate. The car was designed and marketed to appeal either to the family man who would otherwise have had to abandon sports cars, or to the 'older' sporting motorist looking for more comfort.

The Dove was a properly engineered conversion, and, as a concept, turned out to be rather ahead of its time. The MGB GT, introduced two years later, proved that there was a large market for a 2+2 closed version of a popular, mass-produced roadster. However, the Dove did not really

catch on, and in commercial terms must be considered a failure, despite having more room in the rear than an MGB GT.

In an attempt to create an 'upmarket' image for the car, not only were the letters 'GT' incorporated into its title, but the car was also named the 'Dové', the spurious acute accent on the 'e' perhaps intended to import a suggestion of French chic? Pronunciation was thus meant to be 'Dohvay', but both buyers and the progenitors of the car soon forgot this, the later catalogues quietly losing the pretentious accent. The car became, and is still, referred to simply as the Dove.

Although sponsored and marketed by L.F. Dove and Co, the conversion was actually carried out by the old-established Sussex firm of coach-builder Thomas Harrington & Co, which had already attempted a similar conversion on the Sunbeam Alpine. The basis for the job was a

The Dove turned out to be ahead of its time, pre-dating the successful MGB GT by two years. Seen from a low angle, the Dove's high roof-line, necessary to provide a measure of headroom in the rear, is accentuated.

complete ex-factory TR4, from which the boot, rear deck, bulkhead and tonneau panels were removed. They were replaced by a full-length glass-fibre roof that swept down to the rear of the car, the original rear wings being employed after certain modifications. The roof was sufficiently high above the rear axle to allow room for a bench rear seat giving 32in of headroom – enough for two reasonably sized children. Adults could only be accommodated in great pain, and then only if the front seats were slid well forward. A top-hinged tailgate was fitted, the opening of which triggered a rear-mounted interior courtesy light, which was also operated by the doors. The petrol tank had to be changed, a flat tank being fitted into the space formerly occupied by the spare wheel, the wheel itself being positioned on top of the tank. Sufficient space remained for luggage even with the rear seats occupied, so the car really could be used as family transport, provided the children were aged less than about 10. The necessary remanufacture of the fuel tank allowed the capacity to be increased to 15 gallons, a feature that was trumpeted in the sales literature – long-range tanks were in keeping with the 'GT' concept. However, what the literature did not say

In three-quarter rear view the styling of the Dove GTR4 Coupé looks a little cumbersome, but the opening tailgate and rear side windows are good practical features.

Trim in the rear seat area was very neat, although poor headroom restricted use of the seat to children. The backrest folded forwards to allow a longer luggage platform, but usefulness was limited by the lack of height.

The front compartment of the Dove, clearly showing the later style of TR4 seating. The dashboard, with black centre panel, is also correct for a later TR4, but the steering wheel and gear knob are substitutions. The map light is a pleasing period accessory. Front footwells in many TR4s had rubber mats, but it is believed that all Doves were treated to carpet, in tune with the more luxurious image that was being sought.

was that the extra weight of the car, roughly 400lb more than the TR4 roadster, significantly increased the fuel consumption, leaving the Dove's cruising range little improved.

Opening rear quarter windows were supplied, and the door windows were special as their top corners differed from standard TR4 items. The normal windscreen was cleverly incorporated into the conversion. The fuel filler cap was mounted vertically on the tail panel. No external handle was fitted to the tailgate, it being released internally and lifted from outside by means of inserting the fingers into a depression in the tail panel below the hatch. One very neat touch supplied as standard was a comprehensive tool kit, which was stored beneath the carpet on the rear deck, recesses being cut into the wood and lined with foam plastic to prevent the tools from rattling. It is rumoured that the tool kit was the same as that supplied with the ambulances which Harrington also manufactured!

Standard TR4 front seats were used, while the new rear seating was neatly and professionally executed to match. The backrest of the rear seats folded forward to provide a full-length luggage platform, although the platform was relatively

high, leaving the depth of the new compartment fairly limited. Heavy underfelt was fitted under all carpets to provide adequate sound-proofing. Instrumentation and controls were taken from the TR4, but a wood-rim steering wheel was usually fitted. In the first Dove catalogue, this was listed as an extra, but by the second printing it had become standard.

Among the other extras listed for the Dove was a balanced engine with gas-flowed head at £35 and twin reversing lamps at £7 5s. Overdrive and wire wheels were also commonly fitted, and quite a number of Doves appear to have had the 4.1:1 ratio differential, presumably to revive some of the acceleration lost to the weight penalty. All the usual TR4 extras were also available to order, including, amazingly, a heater. One presumes a heater was omitted to try to keep the overall cost looking as low as possible, but I cannot believe that any Doves were actually built without one. Even so, the first list price, with tax, of the Dove was £1250, compared to £949 for a TR4 with a 'Surrey' top (a reduction in UK purchase tax in 1962 explains why this price is lower than the TR4's 1961 introductory price).

The Dove was launched in the late spring of

1963, the firm's demonstrator, registered DOV 1, being much used for press tests, the results of which were generally favourable although it was felt that the car was expensive. Acceleration was rather slower than the standard car in the lower speed ranges, but at high speed it was actually improved, due no doubt to better air penetration from the more streamlined roof. The first brochure optimistically claimed 'with overdrive, 120mph presents no difficulties', but certainly a well modified engine would have been necessary to achieve this speed, overdrive or not. Later catalogues more correctly claimed a maximum of 105mph. Although the demonstrator had SU carburettors, the production Doves almost all had Strombergs in line with contemporary TR4s. There were no mechanical changes to the Dove, even the rear springs, as far as I can ascertain, remaining standard even though one might have expected them to have been uprated to suit the car's considerable extra weight.

Standard-Triumph granted the car the usual full warranty, but did not see a large enough potential market to justify taking over production, or designing something similar itself. This was a pity, as the price could have come down markedly, thus removing the Dove's major handicap. The subsequent success of the MGB GT probably shows that Triumph made a commercial misjudgement, although it must be said that the Dove was not as pretty as the MGB GT, despite its greater practicality in terms of space.

As for the number of these intriguing cars produced, no definite figures can be ascertained. Dove's records do not appear to have survived, and factory build records do not separate Doves from normal TR4s – all Doves were numbered in the usual 'CT' commission number series. Current thinking is that there were certainly no more than 100 made, nearer 50 probably being closer to the mark. Production figures are complicated by the fact that not all conversions were on new cars, for it was possible to take one's existing TR4 to Dove for the treatment. Most Doves were produced in 1963-64, but conversions continued erratically through the mid-'60s. There was definitely a handful of TR4A versions, and the separate 'Dove GTR4A' catalogue that was produced showed that many of the former 'extras' had by then become standard. It is believed that one TR5 was also privately converted, although no TR5 Dove was ever catalogued.

Speculation continues as to why the Dove failed to succeed. The 30% price penalty must have been a major factor, and the lines of the car were also not quite right. The rear view was rather heavy, giving the car something of a hump-backed appearance, although the necessity for rear headroom made this inevitable. Another factor was the

The Dove's tailgate sat, when closed, on two black buffer pads. The height of the luggage platform was restricted by the lateral under-floor location of the fuel tank and spare wheel. The lower view of the Dove is taken from inside the car looking back towards the tailgate, with the luggage floor and spare wheel removed. The top of the flat petrol tank can be seen, and on this sat the spare wheel, fastened by the webbing straps. On the left is the impressive wooden framework holding the fitted tool kit, which, it is believed, came as standard.

appearance on the market around this time of a widening choice of factory-built coupés, plus the growth in supply of sporting four-seater saloons. It has also been suggested that Harrington, which shortly afterwards became part of the Rootes Group, was 'leaned upon' by Rootes to cease converting a rival manufacturer's products. Whatever the reason for its lack of sales, however, the Dove was a brave attempt to provide something both practical and different, and those few survivors are well worth seeking out and restoring today.

Options, Extras & Accessories

The TR had a reputation in the '50s as the sports car for which the widest range of optional equipment was offered, and this continued into the '60s. Although a decline in the numbers of TRs used in competition explains the deletion from the lists of certain 'performance' equipment, more 'comfort and convenience' items were appearing. The list of extras for the TR4/4A, therefore, is as long as with the sidescreen TRs. Gradually, though, the standard cars became better equipped, many items that were formerly options becoming standard on TR5/250s and, to an even greater extent, on the TR6.

The following lists have been compiled from factory parts catalogues, sales brochures and competition manuals. I do not claim that they are exhaustive, for sometimes the factory literature is self-contradictory, but they are as accurate as I can achieve. It is also difficult in some cases to distinguish between genuine 'factory' extras and dealer-fitted or after-market accessories. A further difficulty is discovering when a particular option became available or ceased to be offered, as introduction and deletion points are rarely listed. Most of the following equipment could be ordered on a new car, but some items could only be retro-fitted to existing vehicles.

TR4/4A

The following equipment was available at some time during the TR4/4A production period. It was not all available all the time, and introduction/deletion points have been very hard to uncover – where known they are mentioned. Several options on the TR4 became standard on the TR4A, and some competition equipment was possibly no longer available for the TR4A.

Cast aluminium oil sump kit
Part number 502126. Included the 16 longer set screws required to fit it to the crankcase. Not specifically listed for the TR4A, but was still available in practice.

Competition sparking plugs
Part number 119414.

Lightened flywheel
Part number 132766, weight 21lbs. Included the ring gear. Not listed for the TR4A, but available.

Anti-roll bar kit
Part number 510584. Included everything necessary to retro-fit the bar to car. Not specifically mentioned as available for the TR4A, but it is likely that it was in practice.

Aeroscreens
Type uncertain, but possibly similar to TR2/3/3A design, with different mounting arrangements.

Oil cooler kit
No part number found, but definitely available through factory channels.

Short front undershield or skid plate
Part number 308208. This protected the front of the chassis rails from 'digging in' on rough rally-type events, and also gave some sump protection.

Competition front springs
Part number 201899.

Adjustable front shock absorbers
Part number 143555. These are not the same as the competition shock absorbers listed below.

Competition shock absorbers
Part numbers 113556 (front), 202390 (rear left) and 202391 (rear right).

Overdrive
Available on new cars as an option, and also as a retro-fit conversion kit from the factory. This kit included a new gearbox top cover, the overdrive unit and all other fittings.

Wire wheels
With 60 spokes (or 48 for early TR4s), finishes as detailed in 'Wheels & Tyres' section (page 102).

Alternative rear axle ratios
The normal alternative axle ratio was 4.1:1 (part number 505014), supplied for road use only in

conjunction with overdrive. For competition use, 4.3:1 (part number 502523) and 4.5:1 (part number 503924) were also available.

1991cc engine
With TR3A 83mm bore pistons and liners, this could be had to special order, one presumes for competition use in under 2-litre classes, although it might have been of use in a few countries, such as Italy, where cars of less than 2 litres were taxed at a lower rate. Such engines were prefixed 'CTA'.

'Al-fin' rear brake drums
Made of cast alloy with steel linings, these saved weight and improved brake cooling.

Cast alloy road wheels
Part number 308304. Although very rare, these wheels, with an eight-spoke design, were definitely available on late TR4s and TR4A/5/250s.

Brake servo kit
Indirect acting type, usually made by Powerstop.

Goodyear white-wall tyres
Crossply, of 5.90-15 size for Europe but later of 'Grand Prix' 6.95-15 size for North America (and possibly Europe).

Goodyear 'Motorway Special' tyres
Replaced by Goodyear G800 or Dunlop SP radials (165 × 15) for the TR4A.

Michelin X radial tyres
Initially 155 × 15, later 165 × 15. Other radials were also available to order at various times.

Starting handle kit
This could be ordered for a new TR4, but not, it appears, for a TR4A. A chromed support bracket was added to the front bumper, which was thus slightly modified, and the radiator was supplied with the appropriate hole in it. This differed from the TR3A type in that the hole was somewhat more elongated. In practice, the starting handle option appears to have been difficult to obtain. I know of a one-owner TR4 supplied in mid-1963 where the owner ordered the option, but the car was supplied without it, although other ordered options were fitted.

Two-speed windscreen wiper kit
Part number 510590. Included switch, motor and wiring. Standard on the TR4A.

Continental touring kit
Included cylinder head gasket, fan belt, sparking plug, set of hoses, distributor cover, rotor arm, condenser, contact set, water pump seal, petrol

pump diaphragm, oil and petrol flexible pipes, inlet and exhaust valves, valve spring set, rocker cover gasket and a set of spare bulbs.

Fog lamp
Part number 501702. Later sealed beam type 569908 was substituted.

Spot lamp
Part number 501703. Later sealed beam type 569907 was offered.

Wing mirror
Part number 502459.

Reversing light kit
Part number 510706 for the TR4, which included two reversing lamps, but part number 511166 for the TR4A, which appears to have included only one lamp!

Tonneau cover
For either left-hand or right-hand drive, including studs and fixing brackets for the facia. Available in black or white.

Safety harness kit
In either two-point or three-point fixing for the TR4, but usually lap/diagonal three-point fixing for the TR4A.

Twin sun visors
Optional on the TR4, but standard on the TR4A.

Electric screen defroster
Part number 59844. This ancient item of equipment was still listed for the TR4. Suction type to be mounted on the inside of the windscreen.

Anti-mist panel
Part number 566298. Apparently for fixing to the rear window of the 'Surrey' hard-top panel.

A matched pair of period 5¾in fog and spot lamps, neatly mounted on an appropriate badge bar. The narrow spacing of the TR4's overriders, much increased for the TR4A/5/250, is well demonstrated.

The matching pair of reversing lights offered as an option on the TR4 was mounted on each side of the car in this position.

Hard-top
This was the innovative 'Surrey' top. It had a glass rear window in a cast aluminium surround, a removable bolted-in central roof section in alloy (later steel), and an 'emergency' soft roof section in vinyl over a lattice frame. Normally this hard-top was supplied to order with a new car, with the interior trim at the rear of the cockpit slightly altered. It could also be retro-fitted to an existing car, however, and the factory made available a specific 'Surrey Top Conversion Set' to provide the complete top, in black or white. Controversy exists as to whether cars supplied new with the hard-top in fact received the soft 'emergency' centre section as well as the rigid section. The soft section could certainly be ordered separately as an 'extra' to the whole option, and was probably always supplied on this basis. Other after-market hard-tops of more conventional design were also available from various commercial sources.

Wood-rim steering wheel
Part number 307245.

'Speed' mirror
Part number 573677.

Wing mirror
Four normal varieties. 'D' type (part number 560632) and 'Tourina' type (part number 570409) were 'fly-back' designs. There was also a rigid mirror with circular glass (part number 608467/WL) and of 'Morgan' type (part number 608467/M). Extraordinarily, there was also a wing mirror

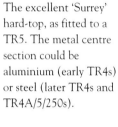

The excellent 'Surrey' hard-top, as fitted to a TR5. The metal centre section could be aluminium (early TR4s) or steel (later TR4s and TR4A/5/250s).

listed for the TR4A as 'Switzerland only' (part number 612306). What exactly was this, one wonders, and was it Swiss sensibilities or Swiss legislation that led to such an arcane part?

Wheel rim finisher
Part number 502160.

Occasional rear seat cushion
Full details are described in the 'Interior Trim' section (page 43).

Leather upholstery
Full details are described in the 'Interior Trim' section (page 39).

Laminated windscreen
Some factory literature implies that this was a standard fitting, but in fact it seems to have been an option throughout the TR4/4A run, although quite commonly fitted.

Heater
The fresh air type, of Smiths manufacture. Usually supplied to order with a new car, but a kit for retro-fitting was available.

Touch-in paint
Supplied in all standard colours, in ¼-pint tins, aerosol sprays or touch-in pencils.

Badge bar
Several types, but Desmo manufacture commonly supplied.

Many types of external mirror were available as options over the years. The 'bullet' or 'speed' mirror, seen on a TR4A, was common, and appropriate for any of the TRs covered in this book.

Windscreen washers on TR4s (optional) and TR4As (standard) were of the primitive manual plunger type. This is a period screen wash bottle and wire holder, mounted in the recommended position on the inner wing. The capacity of the bottle seems laughable when compared with the huge reservoirs on today's cars!

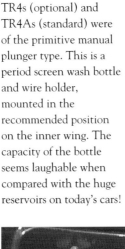

Boot rack
More than one type available, of proprietary manufacture.

Cigarette lighter
Usually fitted below the dashboard to avoid drilling the visible part of the panel.

Seat covers
Various styles and patterns available.

Selmar anti-theft device
Build records confirm that this could be ordered factory-fitted.

Tool roll
A full tool kit was available as an accessory. See 'Boot & Tools' section (pages 60-61) for details of the tools supplied.

Windscreen washers
Providing manual operation, the kit included dashboard plunger knob, piping, jets and bottle. Standard on TR4A.

Low-compression kit
For fitting to engines for cars used in parts of the world where high-octane fuel of reliable quality was not available. A low-compression engine could be specified on a new car, or retro-fitted by means of a kit that included a compression plate, longer pushrods and (possibly) longer head studs. It reduced the compression ratio from 9:1 to approximately 7:1, allowing use of fuels down to 80 octane.

Radio
By the '60s, transistor radios were becoming widely available for cars and both these and valve sets could be had for TR4/4As. There were also sets with a curious combination of transistors and valves. There were many different types, but Motorola and HMV seem to have been the most common – and more expensive push-button versions were available. A 1963 TR4 ordered with a radio from new, for instance, came with a Motorola 808T set, the speaker being fitted on a console between the front seats. Speaker, radio and aerial positions all varied too much to allow any definitive statements on originality. Radios supplied on North American cars frequently carried the 'Triumph' name rather than the manufacturer's name, but this does not seem to have been the case for radios fitted to home market or European cars.

Alternator
The TR4A parts catalogue gives details of alternator fitment – a Lucas 11 AC unit driven by the usual wide V belt. I cannot see that an alternator was ever listed as an option, but some cars were definitely made with alternators. Several police forces used TR4As, so perhaps the alternator was made available primarily for use on police TRs? Some forces used TR4s and it appears that even here an alternator (positive earth) could be specified, although it would have been fitted by the factory's service department rather than on the production line.

TR5

In the parts catalogue for the TR5, only the following options are listed for this model. Where items are common to the TR4/4A list, further details are given above. In addition to the list below, it is probable that some of the TR4/4A equipment was also available on the TR5, although, of course, only where it was appropriate to the six-cylinder car; an example is the anti-roll bar. The heater unit was now at last standard, as were the brake servo and radial tyres.

Door mirror
Part number 622352. For the passenger side, to match the standard mirror on the driver's side.

Safety harness kit
Two-point (lap belt) or three-point (lap/diagonal belts) fixings.

Electric screen defroster

Anti-mist panel
For rear window of 'Surrey' hard-top.

Touch-in paint
Types as above.

'Surrey' centre section canopy
In black or white.

The TR5/250 came equipped as standard with this style of door mirror on the driver's side, but a similar mirror could be purchased as an accessory for the passenger side.

Oil cooler kit
Part number 308367.

Skid plate
Part number 308208. Fitted under the radiator/sump area.

Continental touring kit
Containing parts largely as before, plus two spare injectors.

Wire wheels
Of 60-spoke pattern with octagonal safety caps. Could be chromed or painted.

Overdrive

Radio
Push-button or standard types.

Tonneau cover

Michelin XAS tyres
Radial ply, with asymmetric pattern.

A rare boot rack fitted to a TR250. This factory accessory was designed to pick up on the hinge pins at the front and the number plate bolts at the back, avoiding the need for drilling or marking the boot lid's paintwork. A ski-carrying attachment could be added.

Hard-top
'Surrey' type as before.

Leather upholstery
Rarely specified by now, but believed still to have been available.

In addition, it seems likely that the cast alloy eight-spoke road wheels could be ordered for the TR5, as they were available on the TR4A and TR250. An anti-roll bar was not specifically mentioned, but as it was available on the earlier cars as an option, and became standard on the TR6, it seems very unlikely that it would not have been available for the TR5/250. A laminated windscreen was available to order. A steering lock was fitted as standard for Germany (and possibly Switzerland), and was also an option in certain other European markets.

TR250

In addition to those options listed above for the TR5, plus some 'carry-over' items from the TR4/4A list, the TR250 brochures make it clear that additional equipment was available for these cars, as below.

Air conditioning unit
The control panel for this was mounted on top of the dashboard. The system had two dash vents and two footwell vents.

Cast alloy road wheels
To the eight-spoke pattern, as available for TR4/4A models.

Hard-top
Brochure photographs make it clear that this was not the 'Surrey' type, but an altogether different one-piece hard-top made of glass-fibre. The 'Surrey' top, however, continued to be available for the TR250 as well.

Steering column lock

Special luggage grid
Designed to attach to boot hinge bolts and licence plate holes to avoid having to drill the boot lid. Available in chrome or aluminium finish.

Ski rack
This was an attachment that could be fitted to the boot rack listed above.

Michelin XAS tyres
Of asymmetric pattern and 185 section.

Rubber floor mats

Centre console

This comprised a padded arm rest, extra storage space, a cigarette lighter, a radio speaker and an ashtray. If the ashtray and lighter were not required, a rally clock could be substituted.

Front grille guard

This tubular chromed fitting attached to the front bumper inboard of the overriders, and doubled as a badge bar. The brochure charmingly stated that it was 'to assist you in maintaining the intended design of the front of your vehicle'...

'Touring safety' kit

It seems that this was basically the European continental touring kit renamed for the US market.

Fuel Injection TR6

Again, there will have been some 'carry-over' items from earlier models, but the following options were specifically listed for the injection TR6. Not all of them were necessarily available throughout production.

Tonneau cover

Standard from the start of 1974. Several types, to take account of LHD or RHD, and whether or not head restraints were fitted.

Wire wheels

Of 72-spoke pattern with octagonal safety nuts. Deleted from May 1973.

Overdrive

Originally 'A' type on top three gears, then 'J' type on third and top only from car numbers CR 567 and CF1 (late 1972). From December 1973, overdrive became standard on injection cars, but remained optional on carburettor TR6s.

Radio

Various types and styles.

Safety harness

Static variety (standard after May 1972) or 'automatic' inertia reel. 'Audible warning' type fitted for some markets. Once the static variety became a standard fitting, the 'automatic' inertia type remained available as an option.

Steering wheel glove

In leather or simulated leather. Wood-rim steering wheel, incidentally, no longer available, as a result of safety concerns.

Door buffer

Sold in pairs. Made of rubber, with or without reflectors.

Safety warning triangle

Door mirrors

Various types, usually dealer-fitted.

Wing mirror

With long or short arm, and convex glass.

Panel for mounting additional gauges

Laminated windscreen

Replaced usual standard fit of 'Zebrazone' toughened glass.

Exterior driving mirror

Possibly the same as 'door mirror' listed above.

Continental touring kit

Two types, for PI or carburettor cars. Contents largely as before.

Electric screen defroster

Anti-mist backlight

For rear window of hard-top.

Hard-top

The TR6 one-piece type, made in steel and fully trimmed. Usually matched body colour.

Head restraints

Adjustable type, only available for injection cars from 1974 model year onwards.

Touch-in paint

Towing attachment kit

Oil cooler kit

Steering column lock

Standard on UK market PI cars from car number CP 52786, optional prior to that on LHD injection cars for most markets (standard for some countries).

Skid plate

As described above.

Hard-top to soft-top conversion kit

This included everything necessary to convert a car built with the factory hard-top into an open roadster. There were two types: 'USA' and 'everywhere else'. Most cars supplied new with hard-tops installed did not originally come with a soft-top or tonneau.

Leather upholstery

This does not seem to appear in sales brochures, but it is referred to in the first three editions of the

Substantial TR6 hard-top fixing bolts picked up on the soft-top frame mountings. The factory produced kits to allow a hard-top car to be converted to a roadster, and *vice versa*.

TR6 parts catalogue. It is not certain that any cars were actually originally supplied with leather. I have certainly never seen one. Parts catalogues for CR/CF cars do not refer to leather trim at all.

Carburettor TR6

In addition to the injection TR6 list of options, the bulk of which were also available on carburettor TR6s, the following additional equipment was listed specifically for North America, either as a factory order or dealer-fitted to new cars. A laminated screen, leather gear knob, door mirror and polished wheel trims (from 1971 onwards) were standard fittings on these cars.

Steering column lock
Optional on 1969 model year US TR6s, but often fitted. Standard equipment thereafter.

Red band tyres
Michelin X (symmetric pattern) or XAS (asymmetric pattern).

Centre console
With or without clock.

Chromed luggage rack

Ski-carrying attachment
For fitting to the chromed luggage rack.

Front and rear bumper guards

Alloy eight-spoke wheels
These TR250 items were supposedly deleted by

the end of 1968, but they appear in the list of options for 1969 US TR6s. It is doubtful if they were available, unless unsold stock remained.

Cigarette lighter

Lucas driving and fog lamps

Walnut gear knob

Striping kit
In silver.

Koni adjustable front shock absorbers

Custom-made rubber floor mats
In black, red or white.

Air conditioning
According to factory literature, this was only available in 1971, 1973 and 1974. However, in practice it was actually available throughout the North American TR6's run.

Centre console
With twin radio speakers, and telescopic aerial on front wing (1974 onwards).

Eight-track cassette player
Combined with radio, 1975/76 models only.

Luggage protection kit
Details unknown.

Heavy-duty battery
With 13 plates, designed for Canadian use.

This TR6, a superbly original and low-mileage car owned from new by Eric Barrett, was bought with the optional hard-top. The matt black tail panel contrasts strongly with Pimento Red paint.

Identification, Dating & Production Figures

As with all of its post-war cars, Standard-Triumph used a numerical series of commission numbers with alphabetical suffixes and prefixes, a two-letter prefix generally identifying the particular type of vehicle (eg, CP for TR5s). Somewhat surprisingly, and unlike most manufacturers, the numerical series always started at number one, thus making it very easy to see where chronologically in a production run a particular car fell.

The letter 'L' usually denoted a left-hand drive vehicle, with 'O' signifying overdrive supplied as original factory equipment. For some reason, the left-hand drive suffix letter was changed from 'L' to 'U' in late 1971. Right-hand drive vehicles had no suffix letters (other than 'O' if overdrive was fitted). The 'O' suffix formed part of the commission number, but was always separated from the rest of the number by a small gap on right-hand drive cars, in an attempt to avoid confusing the letter 'O' with the figure zero. This gap was unnecessary on left-hand drive cars as the letter 'L' split the 'O' from the rest of the number. Unfortunately confusion still arises on licensing papers for right-hand drive cars, with the 'O' sometimes read as a zero, thus inflating the commission number! This point needs watching when commission numbers are quoted, especially with an early example of any particular model – a later 'valid' car can be inadvertently created! For instance, a TR5 CP201-O could be confused with a later car CP2010.

Standard-Triumph always called the vehicle identification number a commission (or car) number, never a chassis number. There is no chassis number as such on any TR4/4A/5/250/6 model. If any numbers are actually found on chassis frames, they are frame manufacturers' numbers and have no significance or relationship to the car's commission number.

The TR4 prefix was 'CT', and the first production car, CT 1, was built on 18 July 1961. The series then continued as a straight numerical run through to CT 40304, built on 6 January 1965. A record card has recently been discovered for CT 40305, so, assuming that this is not an error, one extra TR4 may have been built. Year-by-year dating for TR4s, and subsequent models, is given in the 'Dating Information' panel on page 119.

An early TR4 commission plate, dating from 1962, prior to the trim and paint codes being added to the plate. Note that the 'O', for overdrive, is spaced well away from the main number to avoid confusion. The plate was fixed to the front bulkhead.

An original TR4A commission plate, showing an 'LO' suffix for left-hand drive and overdrive. Paint and trim codes now appear on the plate.

The TR4A prefix was 'CTC'. Rigid rear axle North American cars still had the prefix 'CT', but they were numbered in the same numerical sequence as the 'CTC' cars. The first TR4A was CTC 50001, but since CTC 50001 to 50005 were pre-production and development cars, the first true production TR4A was CTC 50006, built on 5 January 1965. There is some confusion over the final TR4A, the last traditional four-cylinder TR of all. It has been published that the last car came off the lines in August 1967, but research in the factory records shows the actual date to have been 11 July 1967. However, the highest numbered car was not the last produced, for the last car actually built was CTC 78684, but three more cars with higher numbers, CTC 78685/6/7, had been built a day or so before. Maybe CTC 78684 was selected to be the last off for some particular reason (colour?), for the end of four-cylinder TR production was marked with a small ceremony and photography.

The well-established practice of assembling TRs in Belgium from kits of parts supplied from Coventry continued through the TR4/4A/5 series and into the TR6 period. These were known as 'CKD' (Completely Knocked Down) kits, but later in the TR6 production run this nomenclature for some reason changed to 'PKD' (Partly Knocked Down), although the cars were no more and no less 'knocked down' than before! Sidescreen TRs had been assembled from kits in various countries, but so far as can be established no TRs were built from kits anywhere other than Belgium once the TR4 was introduced. There seem to have been two reasons behind supplying cars in this form for Belgian assembly. First, many of these cars for sale in continental Europe required particular specification differences, such as lighting or exhaust systems, and it was less disruptive to the Coventry production line to incorporate the differences elsewhere. Second, cars assembled in a Common Market country (Britain did not join until 1973) enjoyed tax advantages when sold in other Common Market countries because there was an element of local labour in their construction. TR6 assembly in Belgium continued right up to 1974, the final 'PKD' car being CR 5498. Incidentally, no fewer than 1248 TR5s were assembled in Belgium, more than 40% of the total, and the majority of the cars sold in continental Europe.

Cars assembled at the plant at Malines in Belgium frequently had extra prefixes added to their commission numbers locally, although the numbers themselves were still drawn from the normal series. For instance, Belgian-assembled TR4As had 'ICTC' prefixes and also 'P' suffixes, so a Belgian-assembled TR4A could have a number such as 'ICTC 50001 LPO' if it were built with left-hand drive and overdrive. No TR250s or carburettor TR6s were assembled from kits, as far as can be established.

Although North American TR4/4As were numbered in the same series as other TR4/4As, they were sometimes given an additional plate by the importer or supplying dealer, bearing the letters 'STC' (Standard Triumph Corporation) followed by the last two digits of the model year. On the paperwork for a North American car, therefore, a commission number may appear in full as, for instance, 'STC 67 CTC 70001 LO'

The manufacturer's name on the commission plate was given as 'Standard Motor Company Limited' on TR4s, but was changed to 'Standard-Triumph Motor Company Limited' on TR4As and subsequent cars built up to the end of 1970. From January 1971 to the end of the CP series of TR6s, 'Triumph Motor Company Limited' was used. All CR/CF series TR6s had the maker's name rendered as 'Triumph Motors, British Leyland UK Limited'.

TR5s were numbered in the 'CP' series, starting with CP 1 as a prototype. The first production

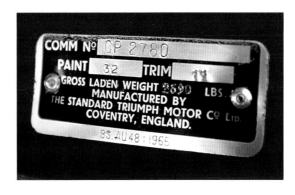

TR5 in the records is CP 2, dated 29 August 1967, and the last is CP 3101, built on 19 September 1968. As far as can be established for certain, only 2947 genuine TR5s were built, even though the numbering ran to CP 3101. It is not certain where the gaps in the sequence fall, but they may have something to do with cancelled batches of CKD TR5s, which were built in batches of 24 in Belgium. Belgian-assembled TR5s have both a '1' prefix and a 'P' suffix in addition to the normal left-hand drive suffix; for example, 1 CP 500-LP.

North American TR250s had their own sequence, based on a 'CD' prefix and an 'L' suffix. The first TR250 was CD1-L, built on 11 July 1967, and the last was CD 8594-L, built on 19 September 1968. Again, there must be some gaps as only 8484 TR250s are believed to have been made. During the first few weeks of six-cylinder TR production in July/August 1967, it seems that almost all cars made were TR250s, only a few TR5s being assembled, and room was only found for these on the production line by cancelling some TR250s! In view of the rarity and value of the TR5, cases have been known of 'converting' TR250 carburettor cars into supposedly genuine TR5s, so a check with the British Motor Industry Heritage Trust against the commission number would be a wise precaution prior to parting with a large bag of gold for one of these cars.

TR6 injection cars had CP and later CR prefixes, whereas carburettor cars had CC and then CF prefixes. The first injection car, CP 25001, was a pre-production example with a TR5 engine, and CP 25002 to CP 25145 were CKD kits, so the first

A TR5 commission plate, showing the weight in pounds rather than kilogrammes. No overdrive was originally fitted to this car, unusually, so the final digit on the commission number is a figure zero, not the letter 'O'. Although a gap would have been left before a letter 'O', as on the TR4 plate seen on the facing page, much confusion arises from this arcane distinction. The commission plate had by now moved to the top of the inner front wheel arch.

'CD' prefix letters identify this plate as from a TR250. The plate now carries confirmation that the car complies with US Federal standards.

Two early '70s TR6 commission plates, displaying the differences between UK and US cars. The UK 'CP' plate records the commission number, trim, paint and weight details as before. The US 'CC' plate omits the weight, but adds month and year of manufacture and a Federal certification statement. For the 1972 model year onwards this plate was relocated to the B-post on US TR6s, and was later fitted in this position for all markets.

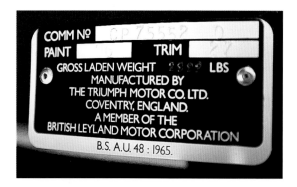

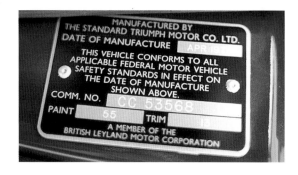

A late North American TR6 commission plate, showing the 'U' suffix that replaced 'L' for this market as the code for left-hand drive. Gross vehicle and axle weights had now been added, as legislation required.

An early TR4 body number tag, riveted to the top of the bulkhead.

built-up car was CP 25146, manufactured on 28 November 1968. This was a good two months after production had begun for the North American market, as the first carburettor car, CC 25003L (25001 and 25002 are not found in the records), was built on 19 September, the same day as the last TR5/250 models. The carburettor

model stayed in production 17 months after the last injection TR6, CR 6701, had been built on 7 February 1975, the last TR6 of all, CF 58328U, being built on 15 July 1976. As detailed in the 'Dating Information' table, CKD cars account for other gaps in injection TR6 numbering sequences, but in addition to these there must have been a further gap of something over 400 unused numbers to make the commission number sequences tally with the known production total. It is thought that this gap probably occurred in the 1974 model year.

The commission plate on TR4 and TR4A models was riveted to the bulkhead/scuttle panel under the bonnet adjacent to the windscreen wiper motor. On TR5, TR250, CP and early CC TR6 models, the plate was riveted to the front wheel arch top (usually the nearside on right-hand drive cars), again under the bonnet. For the last year of CC production, and for the CR/CF series, TR6s had the plate riveted to the B-post on the left-hand side, visible with the door open.

From the start of 1964, when colour and trim codes were introduced (see 'Colour Schemes', page 34), these also appeared on the commission plate. If the car was built with leather trim, the prefix letter 'H' was added to the trim colour number. Commission plates were manufactured by British Metal Engraving Ltd, and came ready stamped in number sequence. However, details of paint and trim codes, and whether a car was right-hand or left-hand drive, or had overdrive, were added on the production line by hand stamping. Later North American TR6s had the month and year of manufacture, plus certain emission control details, added to their commission plates.

Engine numbers on TR4s and 4As have the 'CT' prefix and an 'E' suffix, the number being stamped on the left-hand side of the block, just below the cylinder head joint. Engines prefixed 'CTA' were the rare 1991cc option. Some suggestion has been found of a 'CTB' prefix. Drawing from what happened with Triumph saloons, this ought to have signified an automatic gearbox option ('B' for Borg-Warner). An automatic option for the TR was seriously considered and prototypes were built, but no production examples were made. Factory rebuilt engines were renumbered with an 'FRE' (Factory Rebuilt Exchange) suffix. Sometimes an 'ES' or 'ESS' suffix was used. It is believed that this indicated an Exchange Service engine, which was where a *new* engine was provided under warranty, rather than a factory rebuilt engine under the exchange scheme. There was a gap in four-cylinder engine numbering between about CT 41000E and CT 50000E, roughly in line with the gap in car numbering.

TR5 engine numbers are prefixed 'CP' and suffixed either 'E' or 'HE'. TR250 engines are prefixed 'CC' (not 'CD' as expected) and suffixed 'E'. On TR6s of all types, the engine number prefix follows the commission number prefix – CP, CC, CR or CF. The suffix is 'HE' on injection cars; carburettor cars have either 'HE' or 'E' up to late 1971, and 'UE' thereafter. It is possible that some Californian emission control cars had engines that were suffixed 'UCE', but this is not certain.

Rear axles and gearboxes of all cars also carried serial numbers in numerical sequence, again usually with a similar prefix to that appropriate to the particular car. Gearbox numbers are usually found stamped just above the clutch operating cross-shaft, on the left-hand side of the bell housing looking from the gear lever end. It is believed that the live axles fitted to the North American solid axle TR4As had a 'CTL' prefix. Up to and including the TR5/250 series, part numbers generally were still numbered in the old Standard-Triumph six-figure series (with no prefix nor suffix). However, numbers for TR6 parts were usually of the British Leyland letter and number combination style, although some six-figure numbers still appeared.

Concerning body numbers, all of these TRs appear to have had two body numbers – a 'body-in-white' number and a 'body trim' number. The usually quoted body number, that which is on the aluminium tag on the bulkhead, is the body trim number. The body-in-white number is stamped on a metal tag welded to the body under the left rear wheel arch, in a horizontal position adjacent to the bump stop turret. This number was fitted before the body was painted – ie, the body was in

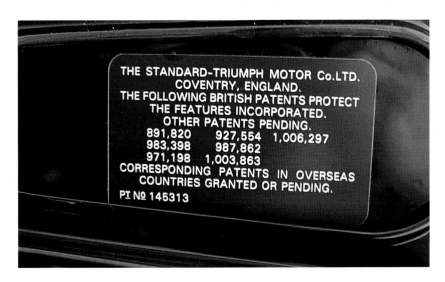

A patent notice found on a TR6.

white – and hence it is usually oversprayed by the final paint colour. There are no recorded details concerning body-in-white numbers, but body trim numbers are in a numerical series very roughly equivalent to the relevant commission number, and they carry a suffix rather than a prefix. TR4/4A bodies have a 'CT' suffix, TR5s a

DATING INFORMATION

TR4
1961	First car CT 1, built 18 July.
1962	First car CT 2649, built 1 January.
1963	First car believed to be CT 18605 (not verifiable as production microfilm record is missing).
1964	First car CT 28709, built 1 January.
1965	First car CT 40193, built 1 January. Last car CT 40304, built 6 January (see text).

TR4A
1965	First car CTC 50006, built 5 January.
1966	First car CTC 64148, built 3 January.
1967	First car CTC 75172, built 2 January. Last car built 11 July (see text).

TR5
1967	First production car CP 2, built 29 August.
1968	First car CP 586, built 1 January. Last car CP 3101, built 19 September.

TR250
1967	First car CD 1-L, built 11 July.
1968	First car CD 2685-L, build date unknown. Last car CD 8594-L, built 19 September.

TR6 (injection)
1968	First built-up car CP 25146 (see text), built 28 November.
1969	First car CP 25159, built 2 January. Last 1969 model year car CP 26998, believed built 10 September. First 1970 model year car CP 50001, built 1 September (CP 50002 to CP 50436 were believed to be mainly CKD cars).
1970	First car CP 50465, built 1 January.
1971	First car CP 52786, built 1 January. Last 1971 model year car CP 54572, built 7 September (CP 54573 to CP 54584 were CKD cars). First 1972 model year car CP 75001, built 27 September.
1972	First car CP 75455, built 3 January. Last 1972 model year car CP 77718, built 21 September. First built-up 1973 model year car CR 169, built 15 November (CR 1 to CR 168 were CKD cars).
1973	First car CR 665, built 2 January. Last 1973 model year car CR 2911, built 17 October. First built-up 1974 model year car CR 5049, built 14 September (CR 5001 to 5048 were CKD cars).
1974	First car CR 5613, built 1 January.
1975	First car CR 6631, built 1 January. Last injection car CR 6701, built 7 February.

TR6 (carburettor)
1968	First car CC 25003L, built 19 September (25001 and 25002 not found in records).
1969	First car CC 27384L, built 2 January. Last 1969 model year car CC 32142L, built 19 December. First 1970 model year car CC 50001L, built 22 November.
1970	First car CC 51033L, built 1 January. First 1971 model year car CC 58298L, build date not recorded.
1971	First car CC 60903L, built 1 January. Last 1971 model year car CC 67893L, built 20 August. First 1972 model year car CC 75001L, built 20 August.
1972	First car CC 78813U, built 3 January. Last 1972 model year car CC 85737U, built 5 October. First 1973 model year car CF 1U, built 11 September.
1973	First car CF 4029U, built 2 January. End of series CF 11572 U. Start of 1974 models at new series, CF 12501 U.
1974	First car CF 17002U, built 2 January. Last 1974 model year car CF 25777U (end of series), built 18 September. First 1975 model year car CF 27002U (start of new series), built 22 August.
1975	First car CF 29581U, built 2 January. End of series CF 31416U, built 3 February. Start of new series CF 35002U, built 3 February. Last 1975 model year car CF 39991U (end of series), built 23 August. First 1976 model year car CF 50001U (start of new series), built 29 August.
1976	First car CF 52315U, built 5 January. Last car CF 58328U (last TR6 of all), built 15 July.

The lubrication plate on a TR4A originally supplied to French-speaking Switzerland. The number of languages used for these plates is not known, but certainly Spanish, German, Flemish, Italian and Swedish are additionally recorded, and there were probably others.

By 1970, US-specification TR6s were equipped with a plate detailing tuning and emission control details.

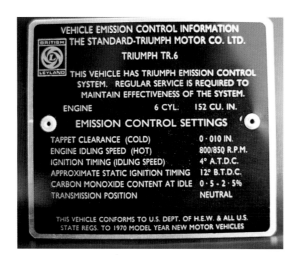

PRODUCTION DESTINATIONS

	Home	Export	CKD
TR4			
1961	10	2448	12
1962	964	14309	660
1963	796	9142	144
1964	819	10657	42
1965	3	247	0
TR4A			
1965	1073	11714	948
1966	1000	8993	1104
1967	1002	2079	552
TR5			
1967	25	29	96
1968	1136	1661	n/a
TR6 PI			
1968	0	51	n/a
1969	704	461	888
1970	1308	1093	n/a
1971	1288	1393	n/a
1972	1720	954	n/a
1973	2002	899	n/a
1974	826	246	n/a
1975	41	38	n/a

Notes
1. TR250 and TR6 carburettor cars were all exported. As far as can be ascertained, none was built as a CKD kit – thus the totals are as given in the 'Production Figures' table.
2. Where CKD figures are given as n/a (not available), CKD cars built that year are included within the export total.
3. The extra one TR4 and three TR4As identified in the build records since the first edition of this book have not been included in this table.

'CP' suffix, TR250s a 'CC' suffix and TR6s of both types a suffix the same as their commission number prefix. Body trim numbers should not be confused with the trim code numbers stamped on the commission plates.

The accompanying production figures have been drawn from the Heritage Motor Centre's records. Not all these figures agree with those previously published, and one cannot assume that all numerical sequences are necessarily unbroken – certain gaps do exist, both identified and as yet unidentified. To pin down all the gaps would involve detailed examination of more than 170,000 build records, a task which no-one has yet had the time or the inclination to do!

It is possible with reasonable accuracy to split home market and export cars as shown in the second table, although again there are a few discrepancies. As previously, the huge majority (90-95%) of TRs were exported, and most of those exported were built with left-hand drive. All the carburettor TR250s and TR6s were exported, almost all to North America, although there were some 'personal export' deliveries elsewhere, principally to servicemen.

PRODUCTION FIGURES

	TR4	TR4A	TR5	TR250	TR6PI	TR6 Carb	Total
1961	2470						2470
1962	15933						15933
1963	10082						10082
1964	11518						11518
1965	251	13735					13986
1966		11097					11097
1967		3636	585	2357			6143
1968			2362	6127	51	1468	10443
1969					2053	6632	8685
1970					2401	9702	12103
1971					2681	10810	13491
1972					2674	10766	13440
1973					2901	11924	14825
1974					1072	11440	12512
1975					79	9113	9192
1976						6083	6083
Total	40254	28468	2947	8484	13912	77938	172003

Notes
1. The year totals are based on cars built, not cars delivered in any particular year.
2. The split in 1971 between injection and carburettor cars has had to be based on chassis numbers rather than Triumph Production Statistics, as for this one year only Triumph counted the two models together.

Production Changes

The following lists give significant changes by commission number (and engine or body number as appropriate). Suffix letters indicating left-hand drive or overdrive have been omitted to avoid confusion. Production changes that occurred on introduction of a new model or model revision are more fully dealt with in the text.

TR4

CT 1527
Early type of console bracket (dash bottom to floor via transmission tunnel) deleted in favour of later type.

CT 2829
Rear springs changed from TR3A type to uprated 'non-handed' items.

CT 3434
Rear shock absorbers modified, and a different specification introduced for US cars.

CT 4388 (disc wheels), **4690** (wire wheels)
Steering geometry and top wishbone pressings changed, 16P front disc calipers introduced.

CT 5643
Automatic boot lid stay replaces manual type. Rear deck becomes three-piece type instead of previous one-piece type. Boot support tubing strengthened.

CT 5656 (wire wheels), **5783** (disc wheels)
Bore diameter of rear brake slave cylinders· reduced from 0.075in to 0.070in.

CT 6344 (disc wheels), **6389** (wire wheels)
Front upper wishbones again modified, as were top ball joints, steering tie rod levers and bottom trunnions.

CT 6429
Bonnet panel slightly modified, incorporating a longer power bulge.

CT 7218
Trunnion to lower wishbone grease seals modified.

CT 7630 (wire wheels), **7747** (disc wheels)
Front disc pads modified.

CT 9553
Integral radiator header tank replaces backwards-pointing TR3A type header tank.

CT 11307
Flat instrument glasses introduced for left-hand drive cars.

CT 11479
Specification of rear shock absorbers changed.

CT 14234E
Open-circuit engine breather/oil filler system replaced by new closed-circuit type. Drum type paper element air filters introduced. Rocker cover modified.

CT 15053
Flat instrument glasses introduced for right-hand drive cars.

15076 CT (body number)
New design of seats introduced.

CT 16800E to CT 16900E
Trial batch of cars fitted with 175CD Stromberg carburettors.

CT 17954
Distributor changes – becomes Lucas 25 D4.

CT 19970
Vent on fuel tank deleted, now incorporated in filler cap.

CT 20064 (RHD), **20266** (LHD)
Steering rack and mountings modified, steering arms and chassis mounts for rack changed.

20925 CT (body number)
Both seats now tip forward.

CT 20310
Window winding handles modified.

CT 21471E
Stromberg 175CD carburettors now standard, on new inlet manifold and with modified cylinder head (511695). Twin oval AC disposable air filters now fitted.

22343 CT (body number)
Change of door check strap from vertical type to horizontal, with resulting door and A-post changes.

CT 23383
Rear springs and axle check straps modified with resultant minor changes to chassis frame.

24576 CT (body number)
Windscreen seal finisher became one-piece.

CT 26930
Hydraulic line brake light switch replaced by spring plunger type operated from pedal box.

CT 28807
Trim and paint code numbers introduced, and shown on commission plate.

CT 29984
Front coil springs lengthened and previous packing pieces deleted.

CT 31506, 31636 (overdrive)
Gearbox and clutch housing assembly modified.

CT 33066 (axle number)
Thrust washers in rear axle modified.

CT 34071E
New type of connecting rod introduced.

37689 CT (body number)
Bonnet panel again slightly modified, details in text. Front wheel arch closing panels also modified at same time.

TR4A

CTC 50125
Gearbox and clutch housing modified slightly.

CTC 52387
Rear bump stop rubbers lengthened to stop trailing arms fouling brake pipes under extreme conditions.

CTC 58000
Fine grain Ambla deleted in favour of coarse grain on black-trimmed cars.

CTC 59836
Packing pieces changed on front coil springs.

CTC 62191
Stromberg carburettors deleted and twin SU HS6 1¾in instruments substituted, still on the same inlet manifold, needles type 'TW'.

CTC 62637
Temperature sender and gauge modified – no temperature markings now shown, merely 'C' and 'H' markings.

CTC 69746
Length of rear springs increased.

CTC 70489
Introduction of redesigned exhaust system with single transverse silencer.

TR5/250

Very few production changes are recorded for the TR5/250 during its short life; those that have been found are referred to in the text.

TR6

CP 50001, CC 50001
First 1970 model cars, incorporating various changes including new design of disc wheel with 15 holes, deletion of previous Rostyle wheel trims, steering wheel changed from black finish and spokes with holes to anodised silver finish and spokes with slots, reclining mechanism fitted to seats. Windscreen surround now black irrespective of body colour. Rocker cover now painted silver, not chromed. New design of inlet manifold on carburettor cars, fuel tank changed, air collection manifold changed. Steering lock introduced on export cars, plus many other detailed changes referred to in text.

CD 51163 (gearbox number), **CC 89817**
Stronger Triumph Stag type internals fitted to gearbox.

51399 (RHD), **52328** (LHD) (body numbers)
Fuel pump inertia cut-out switch fitted (injection cars only).

CP 52320E
Cross drillings deleted from crankshaft. It is believed this also applied to 'CC' engines, but no specific reference has been found.

Production Changes

Many production changes are described in the parts catalogues. This is a well-preserved example of the TR4 edition. Although good reproductions are now available of most of the TR4-6 parts catalogues, handbooks and manuals, it is pleasing to have a genuine original!

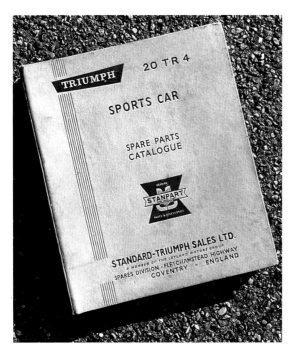

CP 52420E
Seven-blade plastic fan substituted for previous eight-blade fan, still of 12½in diameter.

CP 52786
Steering lock now standard on home market cars (standard on export cars from CP/CC 50001).

CP 52868, CC 61571
Rear springs and rear wishbone support brackets uprated. Consequent changes to chassis frame.

CP 53637, CC 63845
Pre-engaged starter motor fitted (type 2M 100).

CP 53854
Gear lever knob modified.

CC 67893
Carburettor TR6's previous 'single downpipe' exhaust system replaced by 'twin throughout' system. New type inlet manifold on carburettor TR6s. Fuel tank on carburettor cars reduced to 10¼ gallons.

CP 76095, CC 81079
Threads on brake caliper assemblies changed from Imperial to metric.

CR 1, CF 1
First 1973 models, incorporating various changes, including derating injection engine to 125bhp, fitting 13-blade fan (14½in diameter), change of wheel centres from black to silver, change of steering wheel (reduction in diameter from 15in to 14½in), horn push changed from

Triumph shield medallion to 'Triumph' lettering, non-US seats fitted with head restraint facility, redesigned seat covers with coarser grain and fire-resistant material, door and rear compartment trims redesigned, front grille fitted with stainless steel beading top and bottom, black front spoiler added below bumper, number plate illumination moved from top of rear bumper to underside of number plate recess, wiper arms changed from silver to black, heater intake flap changed to a fixed black plastic grille, more substantial front bumper mountings incorporated. Dashboard, instruments and switchgear updated, ammeter replaced by voltmeter, dipswitch moved from floor to steering column, tunnel-mounted interior light deleted and two lights now fitted to shine into front footwells, commission plate moved from under bonnet to left-hand B-post ('CC' carburettor TR6s of 1972 model year also had this modification). 'J' type overdrive introduced on 'CF' cars. New type of Stromberg carburettors on 'CF' cars, fuel tank on 'CF' cars now 9½ gallons.

Note: it is believed that certain of the above changes were incorporated on some of the final CP/CC series cars, but it is not possible to be certain which changes came and when.

CR 567
'J' type overdrive unit introduced on CR series cars to replace previous 'A' type.

CR 5001
Overdrive now standard on 'CR' series cars.

CF 27001
Carburettor cars now had '5mph' protection, with large, black, rubberised overriders front and rear, and new sidelight/indicator units transferred to beneath front bumper. Also air injection fitted to exhaust to reduce emissions.

Notes
1) 'L', 'O' and 'U' suffixes have been omitted to avoid confusion.
2) Specification changes consequent upon the introduction of each successive model are dealt with in the text and are *not* included in this list, which details only changes that occurred during the production run of the particular model itself.
3) The cataloguing of actual production changes in the parts manuals becomes less precise beyond the TR4A, and there are frequent references to changes but with blanks as to the actual change point. For this reason it is more difficult to be accurate for these later cars, so less information can be included.

Buying Guide

From most points of view, the TR lover who wishes to possess an original car in excellent condition would be best advised to start with a derelict but original car, needing total overhaul but – and this is the vital bit – complete in every detail. Beware the dismantled or partly dismantled car. It is so difficult to check that everything is present with this type of purchase, and one can almost guarantee that some parts will have been 'liberated' – and that these will be the items that are hardest to find!

Purchasing a derelict but complete TR is perhaps the best way of ensuring that one ends up with a thoroughly sound and original car, whether one does the job oneself or employs reputable professionals. However, do not underestimate the

cost of a total rebuild, which is likely to exceed the value of the completed car. At least with this approach one pays only the minimum price for the car in the first place: it is all too easy to pay much more for an ostensibly better car, only to find that it still needs a full rebuild once one has looked beyond a shiny coat of paint and new upholstery.

Undoubtedly the most cost-effective, but probably not the most satisfying, way to acquire an excellent TR is to purchase an already completely and correctly rebuilt car. The price will be high, but this is the route for someone who has neither the time nor inclination to become involved in restoration. Obviously, one must be sure that the car is what it purports to be. Before parting with a considerable bag of gold, check, or

High-quality professional bodywork does not come cheaply, but is worth the cost. Many amateur rebuilders prefer to leave the body to experts, but enjoy undertaking the mechanical and fitting-out work themselves.

have an expert check, that the car really is to original specification – use this book! – and is in top condition. Most fully rebuilt cars will have had photographs taken during the process, and a set of these should be passed on with the car.

Occasionally there appear on the market genuine, low-mileage, low-ownership TRs that have never needed restoration, having been cherished and properly maintained throughout their lives. Such cars exist and are usually known to the clubs, but their value, because of their rarity, is very much a matter of conjecture. If you can find one and can afford it, buy it!

Be particularly careful of the cars that inhabit the middle ground between the total restoration projects at one end and the rebuilt or totally original cars at the other. It is all too easy to pay too much for a car that is running and looks smart, yet in reality needs a lot of work. Do not pay a premium for the doubtful privilege of being able to drive the car home. Inspect such a car thoroughly, enquire why it is for sale and accept that it will need more maintenance than a fully rebuilt car – and that ultimately it too will need a major restoration. This is not to say that such 'middling' cars should be altogether shunned – after all, it depends on what one wants and can afford. I merely advise special caution.

As a breed, TRs are robust and rugged in the extreme. Having a strong, separate chassis frame gives a TR a considerable advantage over such cars as MGBs and Jaguar E-types with their monocoque construction, in terms of both ease of rebuild and maintenance. The four-cylinder engines are equally robust, their major weakness being occasional crankshaft breakage. Removal of the fan, which acts as a damper, seems to hasten this problem. The six-cylinder engines are also strong and long-lasting, but can suffer from excessive crankshaft end float after high mileages.

As ever, corrosion is the main enemy, and its extent should always be investigated thoroughly. On IRS cars, the rear part of the chassis can corrode particularly badly, leading to differentials breaking away in extreme cases! In assessing a car, pay particular attention to originality of specification and to what extras are fitted – overdrive and wire wheels, for instance, will significantly increase a car's value. TRs had arguably more extras and options available for them than any other '60s classic sports car, and there is a world of difference, both in terms of value and driving pleasure, between a basic specification car and one loaded with all the 'goodies'.

Research the subject thoroughly before buying any TR; read all the books, join the club, go to meetings and talk to experienced owners. They are usually only too ready to dispense their hard-won advice, and thereby prevent others from repeating errors they may themselves have made. Having done this research, buy cautiously, never on impulse. Do not be afraid of wasted journeys. A lot of TRs were made, a lot have survived, and the choice is usually good.

As to where to buy, the classic car magazines carry plenty of advertisements from dealers and individuals, and some hours studying these will give a good idea of asking prices and availability. The classified columns of club magazines generally have cars for sale at slightly lower figures, but these tend to be snapped up quickly. There are reputable dealers in TRs, but I have to say there are some who are not – and the same applies to restoration firms. One must be cynical and expect to encounter the 'fast buck and tosh it up' brigade. I have always found it preferable to deal with enthusiasts, and particularly other club members. There is no doubt that one will pay less for a given car this way, if only because the vendor will not have overheads to support. However, there is no recourse to a private individual in the event of problems, whereas a reputable dealer with a good name to protect should be anxious to keep a customer happy.

The great majority of TRs of all types went to North America, including, of course, all the TR250s, carburettor TR6s and live-axled TR4As, and since the late '80s considerable numbers of these cars have been re-imported into the UK and to elsewhere in Europe. In the past few years, this trade has levelled off somewhat as values have equalised and the associated costs of bringing the vehicles over have risen. It is true that cars imported from some drier parts of the USA are indeed amazingly rust-free, but it is a large country with all types of climates. I have seen cars from North America that are as wickedly corroded as anything native found in Britain. Nonetheless, several thousands of TR4-6 models have left the USA and now dwell in Europe.

One particular dodge that the unwary buyer must guard against concerns imported TR250s. Several cases are known, and more may exist, of TR250s being fitted in the UK with petrol injection systems derived from scrapped Triumph 2.5 PI saloons, converted to right-hand drive, and united with the registration papers and commission number from long-dead TR5s. With such a limited production run, and with its reputation as the swiftest TR, the TR5 has long attracted a price premium, hence the desire of the unscrupulous to pass off a TR250 as an injection model.

TRs sourced from the USA are obviously best suited to those countries where driving on the right is the norm, as they need no steering nor dashboard conversion, but adaptation to right-hand steering is essential for serious use in the UK. The buyer should always look for signs of this having been done, and ensure that the conversion work has been carried out properly and professionally. Even when correctly carried out, such converted cars tend to be worth approximately 10-15% less than an equivalent UK-supplied TR that has had right-hand steering from new. After all, it is the right-hand drive car that is the real rarity, accounting for less than 10% of TR production. Unconverted cars still with left-hand drive in the UK will be worth around 25% less than an original UK car, and one should bear in mind the considerable cost of having a proper steering conversion professionally performed. Such a conversion is within the scope of a competent amateur mechanic, but, as steering integrity is so vital, this is maybe one area where it would pay to obtain professional assistance. Incidentally, a surprisingly low percentage of US-supplied TRs had overdrive fitted, so more cost can be incurred in finding a suitable gearbox and retro-fitting this desirable option. As for how to identify a 'converted' car, it should still carry an 'L' (for left-hand drive) or 'LO' (for left-hand drive and overdrive) suffix on its commission number, although there have been cases of unscrupulous vendors having new commission plates stamped up and 'forgetting' to add the vital letter 'L'! Later USA specification TR6s have a 'U' suffix rather than 'L' (see page 116 for more details).

In the case of the TR4, evidence of one of the UK 'age-related' registration marks containing letters (inter alia) SU, SK, SJ, FF, VS, YJ or FO is also a clue to a recent import, although there are genuine UK-supplied cars that for various reasons also carry these marks. Post-1963, the registration system changed to yearly suffix letters, making age-related plates on re-imported TRs built from 1964 onwards more difficult to detect. The only way to be really sure is to have a Heritage Motor Centre factory build record trace done against the vehicle's commission number. The Archives department at this organisation's Gaydon headquarters can provide details of this service, which will indicate not only the vehicle's original build specification but also the country to which it was supplied new.

Approach any TR which carries no commission plate with extreme caution, and demand an explanation of the vendor. Likewise be most wary of cars with no paperwork. I strongly suggest that the appropriate Registrars of the TR Register are consulted prior to parting with money in such cases, unless one is buying for spares purposes only. The difficulties of registering for UK (and continental) use a car without papers must not be underestimated. Re-imported TRs that have not yet been registered in the UK should have the Customs form confirming that VAT and any duty have been paid – without this it is well-nigh

impossible to register the car. Pay no attention to flannel from vendors who say that the 'papers are to follow' or offer some other lame explanation. Keep back a proportion of the purchase price in such cases, and only part with it upon receipt of satisfactory documentation.

Caution should also be exercised when purchasing an original UK-supplied TR where no modern V5 computerised registration document can be shown. Even the last UK TR6s were built prior to the advent of the DVLC computer, and will have had old-style registration books originally. Although most will have been 'computerised' over the years, some cars have been off the road for upwards of 20 years and may have evaded this process. It seems generally accepted that a UK classic car that has, for whatever reason, lost its original registration mark thereby loses a percentage of its value, although dealers will often try to gloss over this loss. It can, in certain circumstances, be possible to 'revive' an original number on a car with no V5 document, but in such cases it is better to enquire of the DVLC in Swansea and the TR Register as to the likelihood of this being possible in any individual case prior to fixing a price and parting with cash, as each case is judged on its particular merits.

Almost 172,000 TR4/4A/5/250/6 models were built, an amazing 45% of this number being US 'Federal' specification carburettor TR6s. As for survival rates, it is impossible to be sure, although, logically, the younger the model, the higher that rate should be. World-wide, I would guess at around a 20% survival rate, rising maybe to nearer 30% in kinder climates such as the west of the USA, where huge numbers of TRs were sold. Thus maybe 30,000 or more TRs from the 1961-76 years exist in some form or other, although probably a

The raw material! A sad-looking TR near the end of its first life, with a long way to go before reincarnation.

A perfect bare metal finish is the aim in body restoration, prior to a top quality respray in the car's original colour.

majority of these are not in running order at any one time. It is a considerable number of cars from which to choose, so finding the right TR should not be too difficult. TR5s are perhaps the exception, but even with these rare cars there are usually half a dozen or so good ones on the market if one looks hard. I see no reason why survival rates of individual models should not be proportionate to the numbers built, although models where the majority went to mild climates presumably survive better overall than those models which had to endure Northern European and Canadian winters. Age, too, must make a difference, although this becomes ever more irrelevant as even the youngest TR6s approach their quarter century.

Advice on which model to buy is very difficult. All are cars of fundamentally the same concept, all are available with open tops (Doves excepted) and all have that splendid TR instrument layout, sporty gear lever and stirring exhaust note. The four-cylinder cars are simpler to maintain, and probably marginally more reliable than their six-cylinder injected brothers. Although one presumes that the six-cylinder cars with carburettors should be similarly reliable, there is an emission equipment complication and power loss penalty. Some injected TR5s and TR6s have had their PI systems replaced by carburettors over the years, again one presumes for simplicity, although the trend now is back towards injection. This provides ultimate TR performance and most owners consider the extra cost and complication of maintaining the system to be well worthwhile. The independent rear suspension that was fitted to most of these TRs is also more complicated than the TR4 live axle layout, although comfort is increased. Opinions are divided as to whether or not it improved roadholding! The potential

owner who wants simple maintenance, therefore, should perhaps go for the TR4, whereas someone seeking rarity and speed should consider the TR5. More safety features and modern comforts are found, not surprisingly, in the later cars, and a TR6 can still make an excellent everyday car provided it is well maintained. All TRs, I should stress, remain practical cars fully able to be used in modern road conditions.

As for values, and speaking here from a British perspective, the TR5 is the most sought-after and valuable model – only 3000 or so were made and slightly more than half of these were built with left-hand drive. TR4s and TR4As now seem to fetch very similar prices to each other, although for a long period these models seemed under-valued compared with the six-cylinder cars. The TR6 is by far the most numerous model, and sheer numbers available for sale at any one time seems to keep values artificially low – good TR6s are available at bargain prices at the time of writing! Imported TR250s and carburettor TR6s do not command the same prices as their European counterparts, especially with unconverted steering, and one should avoid paying too much for such vehicles however good their condition. On the other hand, some of these ex-US TRs do have excellent original bodywork, which is rarely found on UK cars.

Optional extras, particularly overdrive and a hard-top, can affect a TR's value quite considerably, and should be given due weight when assessing a car for purchase. Styling differences, of course, are a matter of taste, but from a driving point of view all of these TRs have considerable similarities. A TR buyer should exercise personal preference, and buy the best car of the chosen type that can be found for the price if buying a TR for immediate use, or buy the most complete and original derelict if buying a car to restore.

You may feel that I have been unnecessarily cynical in this section, but I have seen some disasters. It is so easy to end up with the wrong car altogether, or the right car for which one has paid too much, or, even worse, a disastrous combination of the two! As is so often said, you tend to get what you pay for. Decide what you can afford and what you really want the car for – be sure, in fact, that you really want an old car at all, no matter how good its condition. Fantasy rarely lives up to reality, and too many people have lost a lot of cash by finding out too late that they really feel happier in their 'Eurobox GTi'.

I hasten to add that the sheer practicality and fun of any TR makes it a better bet for modern motoring than most of its contemporaries, and if, having considered the negative points I have mentioned, you really do want to embark upon classic sports car ownership, then the TR is an excellent choice. Come and join us!

Clubs

The principal TR club, catering for all models of TR, is the TR Register, founded in 1970. This club is professionally run by a general manager, Rosy Good, and staff, responsible to a volunteer committee elected from the membership, which numbers approximately 8000. The club's full-time office is at Unit 1B, Hawksworth, Southmead Industrial Estate, Didcot, Oxfordshire OX11 7HR (tel 01235 818866, fax 01235 818867). The club publishes its high-quality magazine TR*action* eight times annually.

There is also the smaller TR Drivers Club founded in 1980. The contact address is the Membership Secretary, TR Drivers Club, 3 Blackberry Close, Abbeymead, Gloucester GL4 7BS. In addition, there are several other UK clubs which cater for Triumphs generally, including TRs.

The USA has several clubs for TR owners. The Triumph Register of America specifically deals with the earlier models, up to and including the TR4, the contact being John Warfield, 934 Coachway, Annapolis, MD 21401. The Vintage Triumph Register covers all Triumphs, including TRs, the contact address being VTR, 15218 West Warren Avenue, Dearborn, MI 48126. The West Coast has the Triumph Register of Southern California, again serving all models of Triumph, and the contact is Martin Lodawer, 20929 Lassen Street, 112 Chatsworth, CA 91311. In addition, many regional clubs in North America cater for Triumph TRs, although most deal also with other Triumphs.

Offshoots of the TR Register and clubs affiliated to it exist in at least 20 other countries, including Austria, Australia, Belgium, Canada, Eire, France, Germany, Holland, Hong Kong, Italy, Japan, New Zealand, Norway, Portugal, South Africa, Spain, Sweden and Switzerland.

Bibliography

The following sources (inter alia) have been consulted in the preparation of this volume and grateful thanks are acknowledged to all such sources.

Standard-Triumph Works publications, including Workshop Manuals, Driver's Handbooks, Parts Catalogues, Service Bulletins, Sales Catalogues and Brochures, Price Lists, Colour Charts, Accessory Catalogues, etc.
Various Moss Motors Parts Catalogues.
Triumph TRs by Graham Robson.
Standard Car Review magazine – 1961 onwards.
Triumph TR6 by William Kimberley.
Essential Triumph TR by David Hodges.
Triumph TR4/5/6 Autofolio by Michael Richards.
Triumph TR5/250 and TR6 Companion by Steven Rossi and Ian Clarke.
Triumph by Name, Triumph by Nature by Bill Piggott.
The Autocar magazine.
The Motor magazine.
Motor Sport magazine.
Classic Cars magazine.
Classic & Sports Car magazine.
Triumph TR6 Gold Portfolio, Brooklands Books.
Triumph TR4/4A/5, Brooklands Books.
TRaction magazine – the magazine of the TR Register.

In addition, the following research sources have been consulted: British Motor Industry Heritage Trust, Gaydon; Archives of the TR Register; Coventry Public Record Office; Archives of the Museum of British Road Transport, Coventry; Archives of the National Motor Museum, Beaulieu; Archives and Records of Derek Graham and Roger Ferris.

The pleasures of ownership – and driving. This is the moment when all the expense and aggravation of a major rebuild seems to have been worth it. Do not underestimate, however, the amount of cash and effort necessary to reach this satisfactory stage.